"David Murray has constructed a ━━━━━━━ than just a year's worth of assign ━━━━━━ material you read to your children ━━━━━ *Together* is interactive (thus 'toget ━━━━ Bible passage. Beyond that, there ⟍ ━━━ ⟍ ━━━ ━━━━━ ━━━ ━━━━ thought-provoking one for older children. But wait—there's more! Murray also summarizes the main point your children should take from the text and suggests a simple way to pray toward that end. And he's done it all in a format that can be completed in just a few minutes. If you're looking for a sound, simple, no-prep guide to teach the Bible to your children, you've found it."

Donald S. Whitney, Associate Dean and Professor of Biblical Spirituality, The Southern Baptist Theological Seminary; author, *Family Worship*; *Spiritual Disciplines for the Christian Life*; and *Praying the Bible*

"Many Christian parents believe that family worship is important. But like many, my husband and I struggle to know where to begin. David Murray has given us a helpful resource for family worship that is not only age-appropriate and helpful, but something I look forward to learning from as well. This is a resource that both children and parents can benefit from, and I highly recommend it!"

Courtney Reissig, author, *Teach Me to Feel* and *Glory in the Ordinary*

"Many Christian parents find themselves faced with a very real and very practical question: *How do I consistently lead my family in worship well?* That is where David Murray wisely steps in to help. In *Exploring the Bible Together*, he unites theology and practice in a beautiful and accessible way, all in order to grow the family and bring glory to God. Building on his earlier project for kids, *Exploring the Bible Together* not only tells us why family worship is important but also shows us how to do family worship that is centered on God and his word. I am so thankful that this resource exists to help the church and the family—mine included!"

J. Ryan Lister, Associate Professor of Theology, Western Seminary; author, *Emblems of the Infinite King*

"David Murray makes family worship simple and sweet. Here is a highly recommended, user-friendly guide to spending time in God's word and in prayer with your family every day over the course of a year."

Joel R. Beeke, President, Puritan Reformed Theological Seminary

"David Murray has simplified family devotions without sacrificing depth or quality. I'm so thankful for a resource that is realistic and relatable for both parents and children. *Exploring the Bible Together* equips parents to lead their children through the word of God, learning how to actively read and respond to Scripture. I can't wait to use this book with my family!"

Winfree Brisley, Editor, Risen Motherhood; Contributor, The Gospel Coalition

"Nothing centers the Christian home upon Christ more than regular and consistent family worship. Though most of us know this truth, we find the practice challenging. Unfortunately, the challenge easily turns to frustration, frustration breeds disappointment, and eventually family worship is placed on the proverbial shelf. This experience is known all too well by all too many of us. David Murray's *Exploring the Bible Together* provides an effective tool for encouraging family worship while minimizing its frustrations. It is simple, direct, equipping, and informative—just the tool needed to encourage regular and consistent family worship. Do you need help in family worship? Most of us do. Murray's fifty-two-week plan serves as a wonderful resource. Use it, minister to your family's soul, and center your home more readily upon Christ."

Jason Helopoulos, Senior Pastor, University Reformed Church, East Lansing, Michigan; author, *A Neglected Grace: Family Worship in the Christian Home*

EXPLORING THE BIBLE

Together

A 52-WEEK FAMILY WORSHIP PLAN

David Murray

ARTWORK BY SCOTTY REIFSNYDER

:: CROSSWAY

WHEATON, ILLINOIS

Published in association with the literary agency of Legacy, LLC, 501 N. Orlando Avenue, Suite #313–348, Winter Park, FL 32789.

Cover Design and Interior Artwork: Scotty Reifsnyder

First printing 2020

Printed in the United States of America

Trade paperback ISBN: 978-1-4335-6750-6
ePub ISBN: 978-1-4335-6753-7
PDF ISBN: 978-1-4335-6751-3
Mobipocket ISBN: 978-1-4335-6752-0

Library of Congress Cataloging-in-Publication Data

Names: Murray, David, 1966 May 28– author.
Title: Exploring the Bible together : a 52-week family worship plan / David Murray.
Description: Wheaton : Crossway, 2020.
Identifiers: LCCN 2019027519 (print) | LCCN 2019027520 (ebook) | ISBN 9781433567506 (trade paperback) | ISBN 9781433567513 (pdf) | ISBN 9781433567520 (mobi) | ISBN 9781433567537 (ebook)
Subjects: LCSH: Families—Religious life. | Worship.
Classification: LCC BV200 .M87 2020 (print) | LCC BV200 (ebook) | DDC 249—dc23
LC record available at https://lccn.loc.gov/2019027519
LC ebook record available at https://lccn.loc.gov/2019027520

Crossway is a publishing ministry of Good News Publishers.

LSC		29	28	27	26	25	24	23	22	21	20
15	14	13	12	11	10	9	8	7	6	5	4	3	2	1

EXPLORING THE BIBLE TOGETHER

As a Christian parent, you aspire to practice daily family worship in your home, don't you? You recognize the immense spiritual value of reading the Bible together with your children and of praying and praising God together.

The problem that you run into is how to do this. You've probably tried to start family worship before—maybe you've tried many times—but it always eventually stutters and stops. The three biggest reasons for this are overambitious plans, the absence of a plan, and a lack of spiritual benefit.

Idealistic aims that turn family worship into a mini church service cannot be sustained due to the time it takes both in preparation and in practice. In the absence of a plan, Scripture reading becomes disjointed and aimless. The lack of spiritual benefit results from just reading the Bible with no interaction, with no words of additional interpretation or application.

Exploring the Bible Together is a resource that will help your family establish and practice regular family devotions. It is realistic in its aims, it has a clear plan and direction, and it stimulates interaction with Scripture and prayer.

- It is realistic in that it involves reading only about five verses a day and should take no more than a few minutes a day to complete.
- It has a plan in that it covers the most important passages in the Bible from Genesis to Revelation. Brief comments connect the passages and result in a big-picture overview of the whole Bible. It also provides a daily step-by-step plan to walk you through each day.
- It is spiritually profitable because each day contains two interactive questions for a range of ages, a spiritual lesson, and a prayer related to the passage.

I hope I've assured you that this plan is simple, clear, doable, and profitable. Before I offer some practical tips on how to make the most of this guide, I want to encourage those who might be unconvinced of the importance of family worship.

THE IMPORTANCE OF FAMILY WORSHIP

It is implied in Scripture. No verse in Scripture explicitly commands daily family worship, but many passages imply it (e.g., Genesis 18:19; Joshua 24:15; Deuteronomy 6:6–7; Job 1:5; Psalm 78:1–4; Ephesians 6:4; 2 Timothy 3:15). Regular reading of the Scriptures and praying together as a family are simple and obvious applications from these verses.

It is beneficial for our families. Because God made us to be worshipers, we flourish best as individuals, groups, and societies when the worship of God is at the center of our existence. Worship is a blessing and brings blessings to us. As the old saying goes, "The family that prays together stays together." When we are relating to God rightly, we are far more likely to relate to one another rightly. Worshiping together as a family also tends to improve our private devotions and increase our enjoyment of church worship.

It builds a biblical worldview. Daily reading of Scripture together as a family builds a strong foundation for our lives and creates a common framework with which we view the world. It will also develop discernment in our children, an ability to see the difference between truth and falsehood.

It reminds us of our ultimate purpose. Why are we here? While a sermon or two a week help reorient us, daily family worship prevents our answer to that question from fading through the week. It stops us from drifting into worldliness by constantly reminding us of our need of Christ and of the Gospel.

It leaves an indelible impression. How do you want to be remembered? How do you want your kids to think about you when they leave home or when you are gone to your eternal home? A sports fan? Too busy? A good cook? How about a worshiper of God? Isn't that what we want our kids to remember about us above all else? Many of us can testify to the way the memory of our Dad or Mom conducting family worship was used later in our lives to draw us to Christ. What we remembered above all was the way they prioritized the worship of God and that this was not just a once-a-week activity but a daily reality.

If you're still not convinced of the importance and benefit of family worship, let me recommend the following books. They make a more extensive case for the *why-to* of family worship as well as providing lots of practical tips on the *how-to:*

- Donald Whitney, *Family Worship: In the Bible, in History, and in Your Home* (Crossway, 2016).
- Jason Helopoulus, *A Neglected Grace* (Christian Focus, 2013).
- Joel Beeke, *Family Worship* (Reformation Heritage Books, 2009).

If you are convinced and ready to get started, let me offer some tips on how best to use this book.

PRACTICAL TIPS

I want to encourage you to frame your family worship around the idea of "exploring." Kids like to explore, so let's help them to view Bible reading as explorers view unchartered territory. Perhaps remind them of this theme by saying, "Hey, kids, it's time to explore the Bible!" rather than "Hey, kids, it's time for family devotions."

You'll see that each set of weekly readings is described as an "expedition" with a few sentences mapping out the territory of the Bible that you are about to explore. It's so important to convey the idea of excited anticipation as your family gather around the Bible.

When is best to do this? This will vary depending on family circumstances, but most families find that it's best to do this immediately after their evening meal. Others connect it with young children's bedtime. Home educators may want to use the guide in the morning before they start their schoolwork. Connecting family worship with an existing daily event will increase the chances of you remembering to do it.

Obviously it's best if both parents and all children can be there, but sometimes, due to work responsibilities and other activities, that's not possible. Don't let perfection become the enemy of progress. Keep as regular a time as you can and as many regularly involved as you can.

READING THE BIBLE

So you've gathered your family around the Bible. What now? You may want to pray a brief prayer asking for God's blessing on your reading, something like, "Lord, please open our eyes and hearts to your word." If you do offer a short prayer, try to vary the words each day so that it does not become mechanical. Or maybe ask one of your kids to pray.

Next, read out the brief heading that sums up each day's reading. This will help prepare your children for what they are about to read in the Bible. Then read the Bible passage together—you can use any version of the Bible with *Exploring the Bible Together*. If your children are old enough to read, make sure each of them has a Bible to follow along with the reading. In our house, we keep all our Bibles together in one easily accessible place so that we're not all frantically searching for Bibles each evening. We read round in a circle with each child reading a verse. My youngest is too young to read, so I ask him to repeat a verse after me, a few words at a time. This helps to keep all the kids engaged with what they are reading. You might want to explain to them that this *Exploring the Bible Together* is focused on the passages that will give the big picture of God's plan of salvation and that the verses left unread are not any less God's word than the ones we are reading.

QUESTIONS

I've provided two questions with each Bible reading. Knowing that they may be asked a question helps our kids to read a bit more attentively! The first question each day is simpler and addressed to younger kids, and the second is for older kids. While the primary focus is on the content of Scripture, the second question will sometimes focus on the interpretation or application of Scripture.

The questions help to train our children to think seriously about the Bible and to develop an inquiring mind. They also help to impress the word of God on their young minds and hearts. Although most of the answers will be obvious to you upon reading the passage, I've provided the answers (underlined) to make this as easy as possible for you and to minimize the need for preparation beforehand. It would be best if the children can answer the questions without looking at their Bibles again, but if they are struggling to answer, then encourage them to read the specific verse for the answer.

LESSON

I hope reading the word of God and interacting with it via the questions will provide spiritual food for you and your children. However, to seal the benefit, I've provided a short sentence or two of spiritual application or challenge each day. I've found that most daily devotionals for kids are too long and the kids switch off. That's why I've kept this part brief. Better a little that enters the heart than a minisermon that just bounces off them.

PRAYER

I've provided a daily prayer suggestion to finish off each daily expedition. Each one is related to the passage or the lesson, and will hopefully serve to teach the children the skill of "praying the Bible," that is, learning how to turn one's daily Bible reading into daily prayers. I haven't provided the exact words to be prayed but simply a prayer idea for you to put into your own words.

There's also a space at the beginning of each weekly expedition for family prayer needs, requests, and thanksgivings. At the beginning of each week, ask your family what they would especially like you to pray for. Then write that down in the space provided so that you can remember to pray for this through the rest of the week. You could add prayer needs from your church and also from missionaries. Sometimes you can ask one of your children to pray the daily prayer.

REST DAY

What happens if you miss a day? That's one of the reasons why there's no set reading for Sunday. It's not that you shouldn't read the Bible on Sunday! It's to allow you a day to catch up.

But I'm also suggesting that you do something a bit different on Sunday. It's a day to take a rest from the weekly expedition and focus on exploring the Bible with your church family. That's why I'm recommending that for Sunday's family worship you read at least some of the verses that your pastor preached on and then ask questions such as:

- What did you learn about God?
- What did you learn about sin?
- What did you learn about Jesus?
- What did you learn about living?
- What is the biggest lesson from the sermon?
- What does the sermon lead us to pray for?

This will train our kids to interact with sermons and also furnish them with a framework to help them profit from God's word.

MEMORY VERSE

Each week I suggest an optional memory verse. I don't want to add so much to each week's expedition that it becomes too daunting. But if your kids are old enough and memorization is not too difficult for them, you

11

can encourage them to memorize a Scripture verse each week related to the passage. I've described these verses as "Snapshot Verses" because they will hopefully be like photos we take of family expeditions that we use later to remind us of where we went and what we did. You could do the memorization on Sunday, or you could work on a little bit of the verse each day and build slowly through the week, so that by Sunday the children will have memorized the verse. By the end of the year, they will have memorized fifty-two verses of Scripture! Why not encourage them with rewards along the way for every ten verses memorized, and then a big prize if they complete all fifty-two. What a wonderful photo album of memories from our Bible travels!

WORSHIP

Remember that the aim is family worship! The worship of God is the great end for which we were made and the great end of this book. Try therefore to keep worship at the forefront of your family worship. Yes, we are trying to teach and learn as we explore the Bible together, but, most of all, we are trying to worship God. Teaching and learning are not the ultimate goals; they are means to the even greater end of worship—joyful, reverent, and dependent communion with God. We want Bible explorers to become God worshipers.

Happy exploring!

David Murray

PS. Have you heard of *Exploring the Bible: A Bible Reading Plan for Kids*? This family worship plan is based upon the material in that book. It's an illustrated workbook for kids that follows the same reading plan as this book, with spaces in it for the children to fill out answers each day. For maximum spiritual benefit, you might want to have your children go through that workbook at the same time as your family is using this family worship plan.

EXPEDITION 1
A BEAUTIFUL WORLD

OUR MAP

As we set out in Genesis, we'll see a number of important beginnings: the beginning of the world, of animals, of people, of the Sabbath, of marriage, of work, of sin, of salvation, of death, of God's covenant, and of God's special people. We can't stop to read everything, but if you have time, you can read some of the verses we pass by.

 PRAYER POINTS

_____

_____

 SNAPSHOT VERSE
Try to memorize this verse throughout the week.

Genesis 1:1

MONDAY

Genesis 1:1–5 The Beginning of the World

 1. What are the first words of God in the Bible (v. 3)?

"Let there be light."

2. Who is called "the light of the world" in the Bible (John 8:12)?

Jesus Christ is the light of the world.

 Let God speak first and most into your life if you want the light of Jesus in your life.

 Ask God to send the light of Jesus into the world.

TUESDAY

Genesis 1:20-25 The Beginning of Animals

1. What did God command the animals (v. 22)?

   Be fruitful and multiply.

2. What does the number and variety of animals that God created tell us about God?

   They tell us that God is imaginative and generous.

Every time we see an animal, we should worship the God who created so many of them in such an imaginative way.

Thank God for the beautiful variety and usefulness of the animals he created.

WEDNESDAY

Genesis 1:26-31 The Beginning of People

1. In whose image did God create men and women (v. 27)?

   In his own image.

2. If everyone is created in God's image, how should that change how we treat people (James 3:9-10)?

   We should treat them with respect and speak about them with great care.

We worship a perfect God who made a perfect world and perfect people.

Ask God to remind you that all people are his image bearers and ask him for help to treat them as such, with care and respect.

THURSDAY

Genesis 2:1-4 The Beginning of the Sabbath

1. What did God do on the seventh day? (v. 2)

   He rested.

2. God blessed and sanctified one day in seven. How should that change the way we approach our week (Mark 2:27)?

   We want to follow God's example and keep one day in seven for God's glory and our benefit.

God did not need to rest for his own benefit, but rested one day in seven as an example for us.

Thank God for his loving gift of a weekly rest day for us.

FRIDAY

Genesis 2:8-9, 15-17 The Beginning of Work

1. What tree did God command Adam not to eat from (v. 17)?

   The tree of the knowledge of good and evil.

2. What was the warning God gave to Adam and Eve about the tree of the knowledge of good and evil? (v. 17)?

   If you eat of this tree, you will surely die.

God graciously and lovingly warns us about the danger of sin.

Ask God to give us ears to hear his warnings about sin.

SATURDAY

Genesis 2:18–25 The Beginning of Marriage

1. What did God see was "not good" (v. 18)?

   <u>It was not good for man to be alone.</u>

2. Why does the Bible describe a married couple as "one flesh" (v. 24)?

   <u>God has designed marriage to unite people in the closest possible way.</u>

The Bible uses marriage as an illustration of the relationship between Christ and his church. He is the bridegroom and Christians are the bride (Ephesians 5:25–33). It is not good for us to be apart from Christ. It is good for us to be united with Christ.

Thank God for marriage and for families, and pray for marriage to Christ.

SUNDAY

Read the most important verses that your pastor preached on today.

What did you learn about God?

_____

What did you learn about sin?

_____

What did you learn about Jesus?

_____

What did you learn about living?

_____

What is the biggest lesson from the sermon?

_____

What does the sermon lead us to pray for?

_____

EXPEDITION 2
A RUINED WORLD

OUR MAP

On our last expedition we saw some of the most beautiful parts of God's perfect world. Now we will plunge into the most dangerous darkness as sin enters and spoils everything. Yet in the middle of the darkness, God promises salvation by grace through the promised Savior, who will crush the devil's head.

 PRAYER POINTS

_____

_____

 SNAPSHOT VERSE

Genesis 3:15

Note: _Enmity_ means hatred.

MONDAY

Genesis 3:1–5 The Beginning of Sin

 1. What did the serpent say to Eve (v. 4)?

   You will not surely die.

2. The devil speaks to Eve through the serpent. Why does the devil tempt us to question God's word?

   Because if we put a question mark on God's word, it will make it easier to disobey it.

 We must beware of the devil's attacks that often start by getting us to question God's word.

 Ask God for help to identify and resist the devil's questions and lies.

TUESDAY

Genesis 3:6-8 The Beginning of Shame

1. What did Adam and Eve do when they heard God in the garden (v. 8)?

   <u>They ran away and hid from God in the trees.</u>

2. What should we do when we sin?

   <u>Read Proverbs 28:13.</u>

Instead of running from God when we sin, let us come to God confessing our sins and find forgiveness.

Ask for the faith to confess sins rather than cover them, and experience forgiveness rather than fear.

WEDNESDAY

Genesis 3:9-13 The Beginning of Fear

1. What did God ask Adam (v. 9)?

   <u>Where are you?</u>

2. What did Adam do when God accused him of sinning (v. 12)?

   <u>He blamed his wife.</u>

Blaming others for our sin and our problems is a common but wrong response.

Ask God for honesty to accept the blame for our sins rather than trying to blame others.

THURSDAY

Genesis 3:14–16 The Beginning of Salvation

1. What did God say to the snake (v. 14)?

   You are cursed above all other animals.

2. God put hostility (or enmity) between the serpent (the devil) and his people (v. 15). How can you learn to oppose the devil more?

   By seeing how much God opposes the devil.

When God saves people, he helps them oppose and resist the devil, who is their enemy.

Ask God to help us oppose the devil and his works.

FRIDAY

Genesis 3:17–24 The Beginning of the Curse

1. How did Adam's sin affect the world (vv. 17–19)?

   It made his work and our work much harder.

2. What does it mean that we shall return to dust (v. 19)?

   It means that we will all die and our bodies will turn to dust.

Every time we find our schoolwork difficult or boring, we should remember that sin is the cause of this and of all misery. That's using God's curse on our work to make us hate sin more.

Ask God to turn our struggles into a blessing by reminding us that God cursed this world to teach us that sin is terrible and that we need to be saved from it before we die.

SATURDAY

Genesis 4:1–8 The Beginning of Murder

1. What was the difference between Cain's and Abel's offerings (vv. 3–4)?

Cain gave God fruit but Abel sacrificed a lamb.

2. Why did God accept the lamb sacrifice but not the offering of fruit (Hebrews 9:22)?

Because sin cannot be forgiven without death.

Jesus is the Lamb of God who takes away the sin of the world (John 1:29). Let us look to him for salvation.

Thank God for providing the Lord Jesus as a sacrifice to save us from our sins.

SUNDAY

Read the most important verses that your pastor preached on today.

What did you learn about God?

_____

What did you learn about sin?

_____

What did you learn about Jesus?

_____

What did you learn about living?

_____

What is the biggest lesson from the sermon?

_____

What does the sermon lead us to pray for?

_____

EXPEDITION 3
A FLOODED WORLD

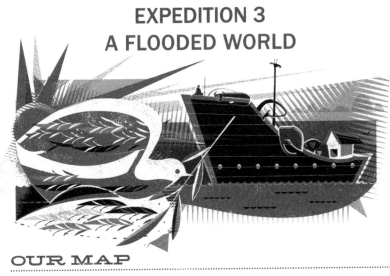

OUR MAP

Hundreds of years have passed since our last expedition. As we look around, we will see lots of people and lots of sin. That's what God saw, and that's why he destroyed the world with a flood. But we won't just see a dreadful deluge this week; we'll once again see God's beautiful mercy in saving Noah, his family, and many animals in an ark.

 PRAYER POINTS

 SNAPSHOT VERSE
Genesis 6:8

MONDAY

Genesis 6:1–4 God Hates Sin

 1. What did God say about his Holy Spirit (v. 3)?

My Spirit will not contend (or strive) with people forever.

2. How does God's Spirit contend (or argue) with people?

By reminding them of their sin and their need of salvation.

 How thankful we should be that God's Spirit still strives with people. He still reminds us of our sins and of our need of salvation.

 Ask God to send his Spirit into our lives and others' lives that we may be turned from our sin to his salvation before it is too late.

22

TUESDAY

Genesis 6:5–8 God Gives Grace to Noah

1. What did God see (v. 5)?

   He saw that human wickedness was great in the earth.

2. What is it to find favor in God's eyes (v. 8)?

   It is to receive God's undeserved love and grace.

Even though the world is very wicked and deserving of God's judgment, God can still give his grace to undeserving sinners like us.

Ask God for his grace, that we may be saved out of the wickedness of this world like Noah was.

WEDNESDAY

Genesis 6:9–14 God Warns Noah

1. What did Noah do (v. 9)?

   He walked with God.

2. How do we walk with God?

   We walk with God by remembering God, listening to God, talking to God, and obeying God in everyday life.

We can walk with God wherever we are: in school, in the yard, in the city, in the countryside, and even in the middle of wickedness as Noah did.

Ask God for grace to walk with him in everyday life.

THURSDAY

Genesis 6:17–22 God Covenants with Noah

1. What did God establish with Noah (v. 18)?

   A covenant. A covenant is a special promise from God that brings people into a special relationship with him.

2. What can we learn from Noah's response to God's command to build the ark (v. 22)?

   That we should obey God's commands no matter how hard they seem to be.

God's special promises to us empower and enable our obedience to God.

Ask God for help to believe his special promises so that we may better obey him.

FRIDAY

Genesis 8:1–5 God Remembers Noah

1. Where did the ark come to rest (v. 4)?

   The mountains of Ararat.

2. What does "God remembered Noah" mean (v. 1)?

   It does not mean that God ever forgot him, but that God had special thoughts about him and made plans for his safety and comfort.

Jesus used Noah's story to warn us about the end of the world and the importance of being ready for the final judgment of God (Matthew 24:37–39).

Ask God to remember us as he remembered Noah and to make us ready for the final judgment.

SATURDAY

Genesis 9:12–17 God Gives Promises to Noah

1. What did God put in the sky (v. 13)?

A rainbow.

2. What does the rainbow tell us about God?

It assures us that he keeps his special promises both to judge the wicked and to save his people.

Every time we see a rainbow, we should remember that God promises and provides peace and safety to those who put their trust in him.

Pray for God's special gospel promises to give you peace in this world and peace in the world to come.

SUNDAY

Read the most important verses that your pastor preached on today.

What did you learn about God?

What did you learn about sin?

What did you learn about Jesus?

What did you learn about living?

What is the biggest lesson from the sermon?

What does the sermon lead us to pray for?

EXPEDITION 4
A SPECIAL PROMISE OF A SPECIAL SON

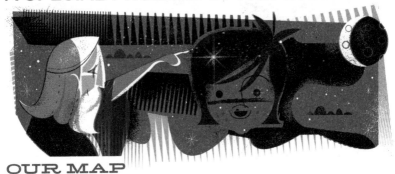

OUR MAP

As the world population grew again after the flood, so did its sin. The desperate situation came to a climax with the Tower of Babel in Genesis 11. God judged the proud builders of this tower by confusing their language and scattering them. Against this dark background, once again God showed how loving he is. He picked out one man, Abram, and promised him a special Son that would bring blessing to the whole world.

 PRAYER POINTS

 SNAPSHOT VERSE

Genesis 15:6

MONDAY

Genesis 12:1–5 God Promises Abram a Great Blessing

1. What will God do to (a) Abram's friends and (b) Abram's enemies (v. 3)?

   <u>God will (a) bless Abram's friends and (b) curse Abram's enemies.</u>

2. God told Abram to leave his country, family, and home, and go to a place God would show him (v. 1). How did Abram obey such a difficult command (Hebrews 11:8)?

   <u>He obeyed by faith.</u>

No matter how difficult God's commands are to obey, he will bless obedience done in faith.

Ask for faith to obey God's commands no matter how difficult they may be.

26

TUESDAY

Genesis 15:1–6 God Promises Abram a Son

1. What did God say to Abram (v. 1)?

   He told him not to be afraid because he was his shield.

2. What does Abram's response to God's promise teach us (v. 6)?

   It teaches us to believe God's word.

It's not enough to have God's promises; we have to believe them.

Ask God to give faith that we may believe his promises and be counted righteous by faith.

WEDNESDAY

Genesis 16:1–6 God Tests Abram's Patience

1. What did Abram do when Sarai had no children (v. 3)?

   He took Hagar to be his second wife.

2. What was the result of Abram's sinful immorality (vv. 5–6)?

   Fighting in his home and family.

No matter how reasonable sin looks, it always leads to suffering and sadness.

Ask God to deliver us from sin and suffering by following his plans not our ideas.

THURSDAY

Genesis 17:1-5 God Covenants with Abram

1. What does Abram's new name mean (v. 5)?

   A father of many nations.

2. How do we become one of Abram's many children (v. 5; Galatians 3:7, 9).

   By having the same faith that Abram had.

Abram is father of the faithful, and therefore father of an uncountable number of believers.

Ask God to fill us with the faith of Abraham so that we can be among the faithful.

FRIDAY

Genesis 17:6-10 God Commands Abraham to Be Circumcised

1. What is the central promise of God's covenant (v. 8)?

   I will be your God.

2. What should we say in response to God's covenant promise?

   We will be your people.

God wants to be our God, and he wants us to be his people.

Ask God to be our God and to take us as his people, through Jesus Christ.

SATURDAY

Genesis 17:15–22 God Assures Abraham

1. Why was it so difficult for Abraham to believe that he would have a child (v. 17)?

   Because he was a hundred years old and Sara was ninety.

2. What was wrong about Abraham's reaction to God's promise (v. 17)?

   He laughed.

God's promises are a serious matter that should never be laughed at.

Confess the times we have laughed at what we thought was the impossibility of God's promises

SUNDAY

Read the most important verses that your pastor preached on today.

What did you learn about God?

_____

What did you learn about sin?

_____

What did you learn about Jesus?

_____

What did you learn about living?

_____

What is the biggest lesson from the sermon?

_____

What does the sermon lead us to pray for?

_____

EXPEDITION 5
A LONG AND PAINFUL TEST

OUR MAP

We're going to follow Abraham and watch how God tests his faith by making him wait and wait for the promised son. Despite many ups and downs in Abraham's faith, and despite a mix of successes and failures, God at last blesses him with a boy named Isaac.

 PRAYER POINTS

 SNAPSHOT VERSE
Genesis 22:14

MONDAY

Genesis 21:1–7 Abraham's Son Is Born

 1. What promise did God keep (vv. 1–2)?

   God promised Abraham a son and kept his promise.

2. How does God make us laugh (v. 6)?

   God makes us laugh with joy when he keeps his promises.

 We ought to rejoice in the fulfillment of God's promises, especially the promise of his Son and our Savior (Luke 2:10–11).

 Thank God for the joy of salvation through the birth of Jesus Christ.

TUESDAY

Genesis 21:8–13 Another Son Is Protected

1. Why was Ishmael put out of the home (v. 9)?

   He laughed at Sarah in a mocking way.

2. What's the difference between Ishmael and Isaac (Galatians 4:23)?

   One was born by human effort and one by God's promise.

The human race is divided in two, those who are trusting in human effort to save them and those who are trusting in God's promise to save them (Galatians 4:23–31).

Ask God to cast out trust in human effort and to give us faith in his gospel promises.

WEDNESDAY

Genesis 22:1–5 Abraham's Son Is to Die

1. What did God command Abraham to do to Isaac (v. 2)?

   To offer him as a sacrifice.

2. How did Abraham respond to this command (v. 3; Hebrews 11:17)?

   He obeyed by faith.

We can obey God's hardest commands by faith in God.

Praise God for giving us faith to do hard things.

THURSDAY

Genesis 22:6–10 Abraham Lays His Son on the Altar of Sacrifice

1. What did Abraham say to Isaac (v. 8)?

   God will provide a lamb for the burnt offering.

2. When has God provided for you when you were in difficult circumstances?

   Ask your family for examples of God's provision.

God will provide for all our needs (Philippians 4:19).

Praise God for providing for all our needs for all our years.

FRIDAY

Genesis 22:11–14 Abraham Finds a Substitute for His Son

1. What did Abraham do with the ram (v. 13)?

   He offered it instead of Isaac.

2. What is substitution?

   It is when someone stands in for or takes the place of someone else.

Jesus is our ultimate substitute, the one who stepped in to help the helpless (1 Peter 2:24).

Ask Jesus to be our substitute, to take our place, to take our punishment for sin, so that we might be spared and saved.

SATURDAY

Genesis 22:15-19 Abraham's Son Will Be a Great Blessing

1. How will God bless the nations (v. 18)?

   God will bless the nations through Abraham's seed or offspring.

2. Who is Abraham's seed? (Galatians 3:16).

   Abraham's seed is ultimately Jesus Christ.

God blessed the nations through Abraham's seed, who is Jesus, and through him, Abraham's spiritual children are multiplied into an uncountable number.

Pray that God will bless the nations through Abraham's seed, the Lord Jesus.

SUNDAY

Read the most important verses that your pastor preached on today.

What did you learn about God?

_____

What did you learn about sin?

_____

What did you learn about Jesus?

_____

What did you learn about living?

_____

What is the biggest lesson from the sermon?

_____

What does the sermon lead us to pray for?

_____

EXPEDITION 6
SAVED FROM SLAVERY

OUR MAP

This expedition starts a few hundred years after our last one. God's promise to increase Abraham's family was fulfilled through his son Isaac, and then through Isaac's son Jacob. Because of a famine, Jacob and his sons ended up in Egypt, where God had sent Joseph (another of Jacob's sons) many years earlier so that he would one day be able to save his family from starvation (Genesis 37–50). God continued to multiply this special family despite the Egyptians' treating them badly (Exodus 1–2). Let's pause and take a closer look at how God raised up a deliverer, Moses, to save Israel from Egyptian slavery.

 PRAYER POINTS

 SNAPSHOT VERSE
Exodus 14:13

MONDAY

Exodus 2:23–3:6 God Calls His Savior

1. What did God remember when he heard Israel's groaning (2:24)?
   <u>He remembered his covenant with Abraham.</u>

2. What does Moses's reaction to God teach us (3:6)?
   <u>It teaches us that we are to treat God with awe and respect.</u>

 God is a promise-keeping God who is to be respected.

 Ask God to give us more respect and awe when we listen to him and talk with him.

TUESDAY

Exodus 3:7–10 God Sends His Savior

1. What did God send Moses to do (v. 10)?

   To bring his people, the children of Israel, out of Egypt.

2. What did God see and hear (vv. 7, 9)?

   He saw his people's suffering and heard their cries.

God sees our suffering and hears our cries.

Thank God that he sees and hears everything, including the pain of our lives.

WEDNESDAY

Exodus 3:11–15 God Reveals Himself to His Savior

1. What was Moses to say to the Israelites (v. 14)?

   "I AM has sent me to you."

2. What is one of God's favorite names (v. 15)?

   The God of Abraham, Isaac, and Jacob.

God loves to be in relationship with his people and to be known as a God who covenants with his people.

Thank God for reminding us of his names and of his desire to enter into relationship with sinners like us.

THURSDAY

Exodus 12:1–7, 24–28 God Provides a Substitute Lamb

God sent many plagues on Egypt to make Pharaoh let Israel go. But because Pharaoh would not let Israel go, God finally warned Pharaoh that all the first-born in Egypt would die. The only way to escape this judgment was through the Passover lamb.

1. Describe the lamb that was to be sacrificed (v. 5).

   <u>A year-old male lamb without blemish.</u>

2. How is Jesus described in the New Testament (1 Corinthians 5:7; 1 Peter 1:19)?

   <u>A Passover lamb without blemish or spot.</u>

Jesus is God's perfect Lamb and therefore God's perfect Savior for sinners.

Ask God for faith in Jesus alone as our perfect Lamb and Savior.

FRIDAY

Exodus 14:10–14, 30–31 God Saves from Slavery, the Sea, and the Soldiers

Pharaoh eventually agreed to let the Israelites go, but after they left, he had a change of heart and tried to get them back. Let's see what happened next.

1. What were the Israelites to do (v. 13)?

   <u>Don't be afraid, stand still, and see God's salvation.</u>

2. What is the main lesson that Israel learned at the Red Sea (vv. 13–14)?

   <u>God saves without anyone's help or assistance.</u>

Jesus is God's Savior who saves us without our help or assistance.

Confess that we cannot save ourselves and pray for God's salvation.

SATURDAY

Exodus 15:1-6 God's Salvation Is Praised

1. How does Moses describe God (v. 2)?

   <u>My strength, my song, and my salvation, my God, and my father's God.</u>

2. What is it to exalt God and how can you do it (v. 2)?

   <u>To exalt God is to lift him up higher than anyone else. We can do this by singing songs of praise to him, as Moses did.</u>

God's salvation of us from the depths should lead us to raise him high in songs of praise.

Pray for a deeper sense of Christ's salvation so that we can lift him higher in our praise.

SUNDAY

Read the most important verses that your pastor preached on today.

What did you learn about God?

What did you learn about sin?

What did you learn about Jesus?

What did you learn about living?

What is the biggest lesson from the sermon?

What does the sermon lead us to pray for?

EXPEDITION 7
A NEW NATION

OUR MAP

God saved Israel from Egypt, made them a new nation, and then gave them important laws. These laws helped them to live and worship in a way that pleased God.

 PRAYER POINTS

 SNAPSHOT VERSE
Exodus 20:2

MONDAY

Exodus 19:1–6 Obedience Follows Salvation

 1. What three things did God do for Israel (v. 4)?

He judged the Egyptians, carried the Israelites out of Egypt and through the desert, and brought them to himself.

2. What does Israel's response to God's salvation of them teach us (v. 5)?

God's powerful salvation should produce obedience and loyalty to him.

 Salvation begins with God's mighty and gracious acts and should result in a response of grateful obedience.

 Thank God for his great and gracious salvation and ask him to help us to respond with grateful obedience.

TUESDAY

Exodus 20:1–7 Obedience for the Glory of God

1. How does God describe himself to Israel before giving them his commandments (v. 2)?

   I am the Lord your God, and I delivered you from Egypt.

2. What are some of the gods that we worship instead of God (v. 3)?

   Examples include money, sports, possessions, pleasure, and ourselves.

God's law is not a way to earn salvation, but a guide for us to respond to his salvation.

Ask God to show us our idols and to smash them by repentance.

WEDNESDAY

Exodus 20:8–17 Obedience for the Benefit of Others

1. How are we to act toward our parents (v. 12)?

   We are to honor them.

2. What are some practical ways in which we can honor our parents?

   Obey them, speak well of them, thank them, help them in the house and yard.

God wants us to honor our parents and all whom he has placed in authority over us, including teachers, police, employers, and national leaders.

Ask God for a respectful spirit toward those he has placed in authority over us, starting with our parents.

THURSDAY

Exodus 25:1–8 God's Glorious House

1. Why did God want Israel to build him a house (v. 8)?

   Because he wanted to live among them.

2. How did God live among people in the New Testament (Matthew 1:23; John 1:14)?

   He lived among people by Jesus coming to earth in human flesh.

God loves to live among people like us.

Ask God to live in our hearts by his Holy Spirit (John 14:16, 23).

FRIDAY

Exodus 34:5–9 God's Glorious Name

1. How does God describe himself (v. 6)?

   The Lord, a God merciful and gracious, slow to anger, and abounding in steadfast love and faithfulness.

2. How does God show his mercy, grace, and steadfast love (v. 7)?

   By being merciful and forgiving to lots and lots of people.

God's greatest glory is his goodness and mercy to sinners like us.

Pray that God would show us his glory by mercifully forgiving our sins.

SATURDAY

Exodus 40:34–38 God's Glorious Presence

1. What filled the tabernacle (v. 34)?

   The glory of the Lord.

2. What is the New Testament tabernacle filled with God's glory (John 1:14)?

   The humanity of Jesus.

God filled the tabernacle and the humanity of Jesus with his glory and grace.

Thank God for his glorious grace that we can see and enjoy in Jesus Christ.

SUNDAY

Read the most important verses that your pastor preached on today.

What did you learn about God?

_____

What did you learn about sin?

_____

What did you learn about Jesus?

_____

What did you learn about living?

_____

What is the biggest lesson from the sermon?

_____

What does the sermon lead us to pray for?

_____

EXPEDITION 8
BLOOD AND DUST

OUR MAP

This week we will travel to two unusual places. The first is the book of Leviticus, which is full of animal blood and teaches us how God forgives sin. The second is the book of Numbers, which is full of desert dust and teaches us how God punishes sin.

 PRAYER POINTS

 SNAPSHOT VERSE
Hebrews 10:12

MONDAY

Leviticus 1:1–5 A Blood Sacrifice

1. Where was the animal to be killed (v. 5)?

   Before the Lord.

2. Who required sacrifices (v. 3)?

   The Lord.

This sacrifice is a prophetic picture of Jesus, the Lamb of God who was killed before the Lord (1 Peter 3:18).

Thank God for his provision of a perfect sacrifice for our sins.

TUESDAY

Leviticus 1:6–9 A Burned Sacrifice

1. Where was the sacrifice to be placed (v. 8)?

   <u>**On the fire upon the altar.**</u>

2. What did the fire picture?

   <u>**God's anger against and punishment of sin.**</u>

This is a prophetic picture of Jesus suffering God's punishment for sin.

Pray for faith to accept Jesus as the sacrifice for our sins so that we may escape punishment for our sins.

WEDNESDAY

Leviticus 1:10–13 A Sweet-Smelling Sacrifice

1. What did the Lord think of the sacrifice (last words of vv. 9 and 13)?

   <u>**It was a sweet smell, or aroma, to him.**</u>

2. What does Ephesians 5:2 teach us about Christ's sacrifice?

   <u>**It was fragrant to God.**</u>

Christ's sacrifice was a sweet smell to God, meaning that God fully accepted it and approved of it.

Ask for faith to smell the sweetness of Christ's sacrifice for sin, to accept it and approve of it for ourselves.

THURSDAY

Numbers 14:1-5 Complaints in the Desert

1. What did the Israelites want to do (v. 4)?

   <u>Get another leader and go back to Egypt.</u>

2. What does Moses's and Aaron's response to these complaints teach us (v. 5)?

   <u>They teach us to bring all our problems to God in a humble helplessness.</u>

Despite all that God had done for Israel, they were still ungrateful and complaining.

Pray for gratitude for God's mercies so that we will never complain so much that we want to turn back to sin.

FRIDAY

Numbers 14:26-32 Death in the Desert

1. Why was God angry with Israel (v. 27)?

   <u>Because of their constant complaining.</u>

2. How does God view complaining (v. 29)?

   <u>He views it so seriously that all the complainers will die in the wilderness.</u>

Complaining against God and criticizing God will be judged by God.

Confess to God any complaints and criticisms that we have about God and ask him both for forgiveness and for a grateful praising spirit.

SATURDAY

Numbers 21:4–9 Salvation in the Desert

1. What did Moses put on a pole, and how did it save Israel (vv. 8–9)?

   <u>Moses put a serpent on a pole, and those who looked at it did not die from snake poison.</u>

2. What is the New Testament version of this (John 3:14–15)?

   <u>Jesus was lifted up on the cross so that those who look to him will be saved from their sins.</u>

If we look to Jesus's death on the cross, we see the sin that put him there but also his salvation from it.

Pray that God would give us faith to look to Jesus as our Savior to deliver us from the poison of sin that is killing us.

SUNDAY

Read the most important verses that your pastor preached on today.

What did you learn about God?

What did you learn about sin?

What did you learn about Jesus?

What did you learn about living?

What is the biggest lesson from the sermon?

What does the sermon lead us to pray for?

EXPEDITION 9
LOOK BACK, LOOK FORWARD, LOOK UP

OUR MAP

In the book of Deuteronomy, we look backward, forward, and upward. We look backward at all that God did for Israel. He delivered them from Egypt, gave them his laws, and led them through the desert for forty years. Then we look forward to the land of Canaan, which God had promised to give to Israel. Finally, we look upward as we follow Moses up a mountain and enjoy his spectacular view of Canaan just before God takes him to heaven. The book finishes with Israel's new leader, Joshua.

 PRAYER POINTS

_____

_____

 SNAPSHOT VERSE
Deuteronomy 33:27a
(Finish the verse at "arms.")

MONDAY

Deuteronomy 8:1-6 Moses Looks Back to the Desert

 1. What were the Israelites to remember (v. 2)?

That the Lord God led them through the wilderness for forty years.

2. Why does God bring difficulty into our lives (v. 2)?

To humble us and test us as he did Israel.

 God leads us through life in a way that will humble us and test our obedience.

 Ask God to lead us through life in a way that will humble us and prove our obedience to him.

TUESDAY

Deuteronomy 8:7–11 Moses Looks Ahead to the Promised Land

 1. What were the Israelites to do when they had eaten well (v. 10)?

Bless the Lord for all his good gifts.

2. What is a sign of forgetting God (v. 11)?

Disobeying his commands.

 When life goes well, we tend to forget God, and that always leads to disobedience.

 Confess the times we have forgotten God and disobeyed, and then praise God for all his good gifts.

WEDNESDAY

Deuteronomy 8:12–18 Moses Looks Up to God

 1. What happens to our heart when we forget God (v. 14)?

It is lifted up.

2. What happens when our hearts are lifted up (v. 17)?

We become proud and self-confident.

 A lifted-up heart is a proud heart that worships self rather than God.

 Ask God to keep our hearts humble and worshipful.

THURSDAY

Deuteronomy 33:26–29 Moses Looks at Israel's Happiness

1. Why was Israel so happy (v. 29)?

   <u>They were saved by the Lord.</u>

2. Why does salvation make us happy?

   <u>Because it is a perfect and powerful salvation that we do not contribute to.</u>

God's salvation should make us the happiest people in the world.

Ask God to give us happiness by saving us without our help.

FRIDAY

Deuteronomy 34:1–6 Moses Goes to Heaven

1. What promise was God keeping (v. 4)?

   <u>The promise of land that he gave to Abraham, Isaac, and Jacob.</u>

2. What does this tell us about God (2 Corinthians 1:20)?

   <u>God keeps his promises.</u>

Because God always keeps his promises, we can put our trust in them.

Ask God for faith to believe his promises, especially his promises of salvation (John 3:16; Romans 10:13)

SATURDAY

Deuteronomy 34:7–12 Moses Replaced by Joshua

1. Describe Joshua, Israel's next leader (v. 9).

   He was full of the spirit of wisdom.

2. Moses was the greatest prophet up until that point, but who was an even greater prophet (Hebrews 3:1–6)?

   Jesus is the greatest prophet.

However great Moses and Joshua were, Christ is even better.

Pray for ears to hear God's greatest prophet, the Lord Jesus Christ.

SUNDAY

Read the most important verses that your pastor preached on today.

What did you learn about God?

What did you learn about sin?

What did you learn about Jesus?

What did you learn about living?

What is the biggest lesson from the sermon?

What does the sermon lead us to pray for?

EXPEDITION 10
ENTERING THE PROMISED LAND

OUR MAP

Under Joshua's leadership, Israel marched into the Promised Land of Canaan and began to live in it. Everything looked great for the Israelites. However, they soon began to reject God's leaders and God's laws. In the book of Judges, we see what happens to people when they reject God and just do whatever they want.

 PRAYER POINTS

 SNAPSHOT VERSE
Judges 21:25

MONDAY

Joshua 1:1–5 God Provides a New Leader for Israel

 1. Who did God choose to be Israel's leader after Moses died (vv. 1–2)?

<u>**Joshua.**</u>

2. What did God promise Joshua (v. 5)?

<u>**To be with him as he was with Moses.**</u>

 God will raise up leaders to guide and teach his people.

 Ask God to raise up leaders for his people, and ask God to be with those who are our spiritual leaders.

TUESDAY

Joshua 1:6–9 God Promises Israel His Presence

1. What did God command Joshua (v. 9)?

   To be strong and courageous.

2. What is the way to drive out fear (v. 9)?

   To remember that God is with us wherever we go.

God commands us to be strong and courageous even when facing new and difficult challenges in life.

Ask God for strength and courage to go forward even when life is difficult.

WEDNESDAY

Judges 2:1–5 Israel Cries to God

1. Who spoke to Israel at Bochim (v. 1)?

   The angel of the Lord.

2. What should we do when God shows us our sin (v. 4)?

   We should cry out to God and weep.

When God shows us our sin, we should be sorry and ask for mercy.

Ask God to show us our sins and to be sorry for them.

THURSDAY

Judges 2:6–10 Israel Forgets God

1. Describe the people after Joshua died (v. 10).

   It was a new generation that did not know the Lord nor his works for Israel.

2. Why is it important for parents to teach their children the Bible (v. 10)?

   Because, if they don't, their children will not know the Lord or his great works of providence and salvation.

God calls parents to teach their children about him and his works.

Thank God for parents who are teaching us the Bible so that we do not forget God.

FRIDAY

Judges 2:11–15 Israel Follows Other Gods

1. What was Israel's sin against God (v. 12)?

   They left God and followed other gods.

2. What will God do if we forsake him (v. 15)?

   Whatever we try, God's hand will be against us.

If we leave God and follow other gods, God's hand will be against us in every area of life.

Pray for help to follow the Lord so that God's hand will never be against us.

SATURDAY

Judges 2:16–19 God Pities Israel

1. What did God do to save Israel (v. 16)?

   He raised up judges (who were like military leaders) to deliver them.

2. How does God view us when sin brings pain into our lives (v. 18)?

   He pities us.

God pities us and feels very sorry for us when our sins bring great trouble in our lives. But he has provided a deliverer, Jesus Christ, to save us from our sins and our sorrows.

Thank God for his pity, but also for his provision of an ever-living Savior to deliver us from our sins.

SUNDAY

Read the most important verses that your pastor preached on today.

What did you learn about God?

_____

What did you learn about sin?

_____

What did you learn about Jesus?

_____

What did you learn about living?

_____

What is the biggest lesson from the sermon?

_____

What does the sermon lead us to pray for?

_____

EXPEDITION 11
A BAD KING AND A GOOD KING

OUR MAP

On our trip through Joshua and Judges we saw how much Israel needed a king. We don't have time to stop in the book of Ruth, but it's fascinating to see that it ends with Ruth's family tree. Whose name is last in that list? It's David (Ruth 4:18–22). That's why we set out into the books of 1 and 2 Samuel looking for a king named David. Unfortunately, Israel took a wrong turn and chose their own king, a man named Saul, who turned out badly. We pick up the story with the prophet Samuel trying to find God's choice of a king to replace the people's bad choice.

 PRAYER POINTS

 SNAPSHOT VERSE
1 Samuel 16:7b

(Begin at "For the Lord.")

MONDAY

1 Samuel 16:1–5 God Rejects the People's King

 1. Where would Samuel find God's King (v. 1)?

Among the sons of Jesse.

2. Who chooses our leaders (v. 3; Romans 13:1)?

God chooses our leaders.

 God removes leaders and raises up leaders.

 Ask God to remove ungodly leaders and replace them with godly leaders.

54

TUESDAY

1 Samuel 16:6–10 **God Chooses the King**

1. What do people look at most (v. 7)?

   Physical appearance.

2. What does God look at most (v. 7)?

   Our hearts.

God is most concerned not with how we look but what our hearts are like.

Pray that God would give us more concern about the state of our hearts than how we look to others.

WEDNESDAY

1 Samuel 16:11–14 **Samuel Anoints God's King**

1. What did the Spirit of the Lord do in verse 13?

   The Spirit of the Lord came upon David when Samuel anointed him with oil.

2. What happens if God takes his Spirit away (v. 14)?

   It opens the way for evil spirits to come instead.

We need God's Spirit if we are to be delivered from evil spirits.

Ask God to give us his Holy Spirit so that we may never be troubled with evil spirits.

THURSDAY

1 Samuel 17:32–37 God's King Is Brave

1. Who is the Philistine (vv. 4, 32)?

   Goliath.

2. Who will deliver David from the Philistine (v. 37)?

   The Lord, who had delivered him many times in the past.

No matter how big our enemies, God can deliver us from them.

Thank God for past deliverances and ask God to deliver all his people from all their enemies.

FRIDAY

1 Samuel 17:41–49 God's King Fights Evil

1. In whose name did David come to Goliath (v. 45)?

   The name of the Lord of hosts, the God of the armies of Israel.

2. What's the result when God wins battles for his people (vv. 46–47)?

   Everyone will know that there is a God and that he fights for his people.

God, who is made known through defeating his greatest enemies, is best known through the cross of Christ, where he defeated sin, death, and the devil.

Ask God to make himself known by defeating his enemies.

SATURDAY

1 Samuel 17:50–54 God's King Wins

1. What did David not use to defeat Goliath (v. 50)?

A sword.

2. Who is your greatest enemy?

The devil, also known as Satan.

God can use the greatest weapon of his greatest enemies to defeat his enemies, just as he did by using the cross of Christ to defeat his greatest spiritual enemies (Colossians 2:14–15).

Thank God for his defeat of the devil at the cross

SUNDAY

Read the most important verses that your pastor preached on today.

What did you learn about God?

What did you learn about sin?

What did you learn about Jesus?

What did you learn about living?

What is the biggest lesson from the sermon?

What does the sermon lead us to pray for?

EXPEDITION 12
A SPECIAL PROMISE OF A SPECIAL KING

OUR MAP

David was Israel's greatest king, and we'd love to spend time exploring the details of his life. But because we need to keep moving, our explorations will have to pick the most important events. This week we're going to look at the highest point in his life—the special covenant promises God gave him. Then we're going to look at the lowest point in David's life—when he committed terrible sins.

 PRAYER POINTS

 SNAPSHOT VERSE
2 Samuel 7:16

MONDAY

2 Samuel 7:12–17 God Makes Great Promises

 1. What does God promise David (v. 16)?

A kingdom and throne that would last forever.

2. How was this promise fulfilled (Luke 1:32–33)?

Jesus, the Son of David, set up an everlasting spiritual kingdom.

 God's kingdom is an everlasting kingdom that can never be stopped.

 Thank God for King Jesus and pray that his kingdom would come more and more upon the earth.

TUESDAY

2 Samuel 7:18–24 David Humbly Replies

1. What question does David ask (v. 18)?

   Who am I and what is my house?

2. What does David's response teach us about how we should respond to God's gracious promises?

   We should react with humble amazement at God's grace.

True worship begins with humility, with a sense of wonder that God should be so kind to us.

Ask God for the humility of heart that is amazed at God's saving mercies.

WEDNESDAY

2 Samuel 11:1–5 David Sins

1. Which commandment did David break (Exodus 20:14)?

   The command not to commit adultery.

2. How did David's sin begin (v. 2)?

   It began when David watched a woman bathing.

We must beware of how a smaller sin can quickly become a much bigger sin.

Pray "do not lead us into temptation, but deliver us from evil" (Matthew 6:13).

THURSDAY

2 Samuel 12:1–6 Nathan Illustrates David's Sin

1. In what way is David like the rich man in Nathan's story (v. 4)?

   <u>He stole another man's wife when he already had one himself.</u>

2. What does David's response to Nathan's story teach us (vv. 5–6)?

   <u>We can be outraged and angry at others' sins but ignore or excuse our own.</u>

We can be blind to our worst sins but be very critical of them when we see them in others.

Thank God for faithful pastors who show us our sins, and pray that we will be more angry with our sins than others' sins.

FRIDAY

2 Samuel 12:7–10 Nathan Uncovers David's Sin

1. What was God's punishment for David's sins (v. 10)?

   <u>The sword will never leave his house.</u>

2. What can happen to private sins (v. 12)?

   <u>God can make very public what we did in secret.</u>

Private sins can have very public and painful consequences.

Ask that God would keep us from committing sin and therefore the terrible consequences that can follow.

SATURDAY

2 Samuel 12:11–14 David Confesses His Sin

1. What did Nathan say to David (v. 13)?

   God has put away your sin.

2. What was one result of David's sin (v. 14)?

   Because David's sin had caused God's enemies to blaspheme, David's child would die.

Even when God forgives our sins, so that we will not go to hell, there may be painful consequences in this world, so that others will not follow our sins.

Pray for forgiveness of sins, but also acceptance of any earthly consequences that may follow our sins.

SUNDAY

Read the most important verses that your pastor preached on today.

What did you learn about God?

What did you learn about sin?

What did you learn about Jesus?

What did you learn about living?

What is the biggest lesson from the sermon?

What does the sermon lead us to pray for?

EXPEDITION 13
SONGS IN THE MIDST OF SADNESS

OUR MAP

When you sin against your mom or dad, they may have to discipline you even though they still love you. Actually, they discipline you *because* they love you. That's what we see God doing in the remaining chapters of David's life. Because God still loves him, God disciplines David with a number of sad events in his life. This includes the rebellion of his son, Absalom, which ends in Absalom's death. However, at the end of his life, we will hear David sing a beautiful song of praise to God and then some beautiful words of trust in God's promises of a greater and everlasting King.

 PRAYER POINTS

 SNAPSHOT VERSE
2 Samuel 22:47

MONDAY

2 Samuel 18:5, 9–10, 14–15 David's Son Is Killed

1. Absalom wanted to kill his father, David. Even so, what did David ask Joab to do with Absalom (v. 5)?

   Be gentle with Absalom.

2. What do we learn from Absalom's rebellion (vv. 14–15; Exodus 20:12)?

   We learn that dishonoring our parents can result in an early death.

 Rebellion against God's authorities in our lives can shorten our lives.

 Let us confess any rebellion against our parents and pray for help to honor them, so that our lives may last longer and be happier.

TUESDAY

2 Samuel 18:33–19:4 David Weeps Over His Son

1. What did David say when he heard that Absalom was dead (18:33)?

   He wished he had died in the place of Absalom.

2. In what way is David's spirit here similar to Jesus Christ (Romans 5:8)?

   Jesus not only wished to die in place of rebels and enemies, but did so.

David could not die in place of his son Absalom, but David's greatest son, Jesus Christ, died in place of David and all who put their trust in the Savior.

Ask Jesus to be your substitute, that his death would be in your place.

WEDNESDAY

2 Samuel 22:1–4 David Sings to God His Rock

1. What does David call God (v. 2)?

   A rock, a fortress, and a deliverer.

2. In what ways has God been your shield (v. 3)?

   Talk about the ways in which God has protected you throughout your life.

We need God to defend and protect us every day of our lives.

Praise God for the many times and ways in which he has defended us.

THURSDAY

2 Samuel 22:31–36 David Sings to God His Shield

1. What does David say about God's word at the end of his life (v. 31)?

   It has been proved true again and again.

2. How has God's word been proved true in your own life?

   Talk about ways in which God's word came true in your life and your family's life.

God's word has been proven true by many people in many places over many years.

Thank God for his reliable word and pray for its fulfillment.

FRIDAY

2 Samuel 22:47–51 David Sings to God His Salvation

1. What does David say he will do (v. 50)?

   He will give praise to God among the nations.

2. Where can you witness to God's goodness?

   At school, among my friends, with my teammates, or with my neighbors.

God calls us to be his witnesses in the world, to make him known to those who do not know him.

Ask God for courage to be his witnesses wherever we go.

SATURDAY

2 Samuel 23:1–5 David Trusts in God's Promises

1. What is David's hope (v. 5)?

   God's everlasting covenant.

2. How does David describe this covenant (v. 5)?

   It is organized, secure, and saving.

Our only hope of salvation is God's covenant promises, which are ultimately fulfilled in Jesus Christ (Luke 22:20).

Pray for David-like trust in God's everlasting covenant promises, which have been secured by Christ's blood.

SUNDAY

Read the most important verses that your pastor preached on today.

What did you learn about God?

What did you learn about sin?

What did you learn about Jesus?

What did you learn about living?

What is the biggest lesson from the sermon?

What does the sermon lead us to pray for?

EXPEDITION 14
A CAPTIVE NATION

OUR MAP

Our map of the next four books of Kings and Chronicles looks messy. It's messy because the lives of Israel's kings were messy. Like King David, his son Solomon started his reign well: he built a temple for God. But he also fell into terrible sin. Just as sin separated King David's family, so sin separated King Solomon's kingdom into two parts—Israel and Judah. And as the kings and people kept on sinning, God finally separated them from the land. He sent enemies like Babylon to invade, capture the people, and take them back to Babylon as prisoners.

 PRAYER POINTS

 SNAPSHOT VERSE
1 Kings 8:56

MONDAY

1 Kings 8:14–21 Solomon Worships God

 1. What did David want to do (v. 17)?

He wanted to build God a house (a temple).

2. What did God say to David (vv. 18–19)?

Your desire to build the house is good but your son will do it instead.

 Our rule for obedience is not our good desires but God's will.

 Ask God to help us accept the roles he has for us in life, even if they do not match our best desires.

TUESDAY

1 Kings 11:1–6 Solomon Worships Idols

1. How did Solomon compare with his father David (v. 6)?

   He did not follow the Lord as fully as David.

2. What are the specific sins that Solomon committed and we are to avoid (vv. 1–5)?

   We are to avoid marrying ungodly people and worshiping their idols.

God forbids his people from marrying ungodly partners (1 Corinthians 7:39; 2 Corinthians 6:14).

Ask God to prepare and provide godly husbands and wives for his people.

WEDNESDAY

1 Kings 11:7–13 God Punishes Solomon

1. How did God punish Solomon for his sins (v. 11)?

   God took some of the kingdom away from Solomon.

2. Why did God not take the whole kingdom away from Solomon (v. 13)?

   Because of the covenant promises God gave to David.

Because of Jesus, God punishes us less than we deserve for our sins.

Thank God for his mercy in Christ, even when he punishes us for our sins.

THURSDAY

2 Chronicles 36:11–16 Judah's Last King

1. What did Israel do to God's temple (v. 14)?

   They defiled it.

2. What motivates God to send messengers to warn his people about their sins (v. 15)?

   His compassion and pity for them.

God's compassion and pity are behind his warnings about sin that we hear from our pastors.

Pray for humble hearts to receive God's compassionate warnings about sin.

FRIDAY

2 Chronicles 36:16–21 Judah's Punishment

1. Why did God eventually carry his people into Babylon (v. 16)?

   Because they mocked God's prophets and laughed at them.

2. How are you reacting to God's messages of warning through your pastors or your parents?

   Humble repentance, or defiance and mocking.

While God is patient and compassionate in warning us about sin and calling us to repentance, there is a limit, and, when reached, God has to act to punish.

Confess if we have ever laughed at or rejected God's warnings and pray for help to hear and respond with humility and repentance in order to avoid judgment.

SATURDAY

2 Chronicles 36:22-23 Judah's Hope

 1. Who made King Cyrus release the people (v. 22)?

The Lord's Spirit stirred the spirit of Cyrus.

2. What happened after God's people were held captive in Babylon for seventy years (v. 23)?

King Cyrus released them and sent them back to Jerusalem to rebuild the temple.

 Even when all seems lost, God can act to give his people hope of a bright future.

 Pray for hope in darkest times, trusting that God will bring light into the darkness and good out of evil.

God had promised a godly king ruling over a godly people in a godly kingdom. Many kings, many chapters, and many miles later, we seem no closer to seeing this promise fulfilled. However, Saturday's reading should give us hope that our exploration may yet have a happy ending. Second Chronicles 36:22-23 describes what happened after God's people and God's king had been held prisoners in Babylon for seventy years. What does this tell you about God's promises? Can you think of another time of surprising hope when all seemed lost? Here's a clue: Mark 16:1-8.

SUNDAY

Read the most important verses that your pastor preached on today.

 What did you learn about God?

What did you learn about sin?

What did you learn about Jesus?

What did you learn about living?

What is the biggest lesson from the sermon?

What does the sermon lead us to pray for?

EXPEDITION 15
A REBUILT NATION

OUR MAP

We are ready to start our expedition into the book of Ezra. God has moved the heathen King Cyrus to release God's people, allowing them to return to Jerusalem and rebuild the city and temple. Ezra and the people rebuild the temple. However, despite this progress there's still disappointment because the temple is much smaller than before, the people are still sinning, and there still is no king.

 PRAYER POINTS

 SNAPSHOT VERSE
Ezra 7:27

MONDAY

Ezra 1:1–4 Cyrus Plans to Rebuild the Temple

 1. Who gave King Cyrus his power (v. 2)?

The Lord God of heaven.

2. What did Cyrus say to God's people (v. 3)?

Go up to Jerusalem and rebuild God's house.

 God can access the hearts of heathen kings and make them do his will for the good of God's kingdom and people.

 Pray for our leaders, that even if they are not Christians, God would access their hearts and direct them to make decisions for the good of God's kingdom and people.

TUESDAY

Ezra 3:8-13 The People Build the Temple

1. What did the priests sing when the temple-building began (v. 11)?

   God is good and his love lasts forever.

2. What did the people do (v. 11)?

   They shouted with a great shout.

Our praise for God's gracious acts should be loud and enthusiastic.

Praise God loudly for his goodness and mercy.

WEDNESDAY

Ezra 9:1-4 The People Sin

1. What did Ezra do when he heard the people had started marrying the heathen (v. 3)?

   He tore his clothes, plucked out his beard, and sat astonished.

2. What does Ezra's reaction tell us about the sin of marrying non-Christians?

   That it is one of the most serious sins in God's eyes.

Sin should be a horror to us; we should be astonished at it in our lives and the lives of others.

Ask God to give us a horror of all sin, including that of Christians marrying non-Christians.

THURSDAY

Ezra 9:5–9 Ezra Confesses the People's Sins

1. What position did Ezra take before God (v. 5)?

   He fell on his knees and spread out his hands to God.

2. How great are our sins (v. 6)?

   They rise above our heads and even as high as the heavens.

The greatness of sin should humble us before God.

Ask God for help to see how great sin is and how low we should be before God as we confess it.

FRIDAY

Ezra 9:10–15 Ezra Pleads for Mercy

1. How had God punished the people (v. 13)?

   Less than they deserved.

2. Have you ever been punished for your sins as you deserved?

   No, always less than we deserved.

Jesus was the only one who was ever punished as sin deserved, and that was not for any sins he had committed.

Thank God that he has never punished us as we deserved, and praise him that he has punished Jesus as sin deserved in order to free us from our deserved punishment.

SATURDAY

Ezra 10:1–4 The People Confess Their Sins

1. How did the people respond to God's commandment (v. 3)?

   They promised to put away their ungodly wives.

2. What sins will you promise to put away today?

   Ask one another to identify sins to put away.

If we confess *and* forsake our sins, we will find mercy (Proverbs 28:13).

Pray for a spirit of true confession and covenanting to put away every sin.

SUNDAY

Read the most important verses that your pastor preached on today.

What did you learn about God?

What did you learn about sin?

What did you learn about Jesus?

What did you learn about living?

What is the biggest lesson from the sermon?

What does the sermon lead us to pray for?

EXPEDITION 16
THE DEVIL ATTACKS

OUR MAP

We've now traveled over three thousand years since we started our expedition in Genesis! We've covered a lot of miles and discovered many evidences of God's love to sinners. Despite Adam's sin, God promised a King who would destroy sin and save his people. And despite the Israelites' constant sinning, God's promise still stands. We're going to pause now and travel backward a bit to look at how various poets and prophets wrote about their hope for deliverance by God's King. We'll start with Job, a man whom the devil attacked so badly that he lost his home, his family, his wealth, and his health. But did he give up hope in God? Let's see.

 PRAYER POINTS

 SNAPSHOT VERSE
Job 19:25

MONDAY

Job 1:1–5 A Godly Man

 1. Describe Job's character (v. 1).

He was blameless, upright, feared God, and turned away from evil.

2. Job offered sacrifices for his family because he was afraid they might have cursed God in their hearts (v. 5). What can we do for family members who may have sinned?

We can pray for them.

 We need to pray for one another in our families lest any of us sin against God.

 Ask God to keep each member of our family from sin, especially the sin of dishonoring God.

TUESDAY

Job 1:6-12 A Targeted Man

1. What did Satan say Job would do (v. 11)?

   He said that Job would curse God if God let bad things happen to him.

2. Who controls the devil (vv. 7, 12)?

   God is in ultimate control of the devil, as he cannot do anything without God's permission.

The devil can do nothing against God's people without God's permission.

Thank God for his control of the devil, and pray that he would daily deliver us from evil.

WEDNESDAY

Job 1:13-19 A Suffering Man

1. Who was killed by the great wind (vv. 18-19)?

   Job's sons and daughters.

2. Who is to be blamed for terrible tragedies?

   The devil.

We must trace all evil to the devil's hostility against God as his enemy.

Pray that God would use tragedies to make us oppose sin and the devil more.

THURSDAY

Job 1:20–22 A Worshiping Man

1. How did Job react to the tragedies (v. 20)?

   He tore his clothes, shaved his head, fell to the ground, and worshiped God.

2. Who is in ultimate control of what we have in this life (v. 21)?

   God gives, and God takes away.

Job is a perfect example of how to respond to trouble: he did not sin but worshiped and submitted to God.

Pray for Job-like worship and submission when difficulties come into our lives.

FRIDAY

Job 19:23–27 A Hope-Filled Man

1. What did Job know (v. 25)?

   He knew that his Redeemer was alive and would one day stand on the earth.

2. How is Job's hope like the Christian's hope (v. 26)?

   Like the Christian, Job knew he would die and his flesh would turn to dust, but he also knew he would be resurrected and in his flesh he would see God.

If God is our Redeemer, he will save us from death and bring us into his presence.

Ask God to take away the fear of death and give us confidence of a resurrection life in the world to come.

Bridge: In chapters 4–37, Job's friends gave him a lot of bad counsel. Job sometimes reacted badly to this advice. However, when God gives his perfect counsel in chapters 38–41, Job was humbled.

SATURDAY

Job 42:10–16 A Restored Man

1. What did God give Job when his suffering ended (v. 10)?

Twice as much as he had before.

2. How is Job an example for how we should treat people who harm us (v. 10)?

Job is an example in how he prayed for people who had treated him badly.

Job experienced a mini-resurrection, which was a small picture of the great resurrection all God's people will experience (John 11:25; 1 Corinthians 15:20–22).

Pray that God's suffering people will keep their resurrection hopes alive in the midst of trials.

SUNDAY

Read the most important verses that your pastor preached on today.

What did you learn about God?

What did you learn about sin?

What did you learn about Jesus?

What did you learn about living?

What is the biggest lesson from the sermon?

What does the sermon lead us to pray for?

EXPEDITION 17
SONGS ABOUT THE COMING KING

OUR MAP

Get your headphones on because for the next two weeks we're going to be listening to the songs God gave to his people to sing while they waited for the coming King. These songs have an unusual combination: the King is opposed, the King suffers, and the King is victorious. As you listen to these songs, think about who matches this description: an opposed King, a suffering King, and a victorious King.

 PRAYER POINTS

 SNAPSHOT VERSE
Psalm 2:12

_____

_____

MONDAY

Psalm 2:1–6 The King Is Opposed

 1. Who opposes God's King (v. 2)?

The kings and rulers of the earth.

2. What does it mean when it says that God laughs at those who oppose him (v. 4)?

It means that God is not threatened or worried by opposition to him.

 Even when many powerful people oppose God, God is not worried but remains in total control.

 Pray for trust in God's sovereignty, especially when we see so many trying to overthrow his kingdom.

TUESDAY

Psalm 2:7–12 The King Is Victorious

1. What will the King do to his enemies (v. 9)?

   <u>He will dash them to pieces.</u>

2. How do we "kiss the Son" (v. 12)?

   <u>By loving God's Son, Jesus Christ.</u>

We are either opponents of Jesus Christ or lovers of Jesus Christ.

Ask God to turn us from being haters to being lovers of Jesus.

WEDNESDAY

Psalm 22:1–5 The King Is Forsaken by God

1. What is the first question the suffering King asks God in this psalm (v. 1)?

   <u>"Why have you forsaken me?"</u>

2. What does the suffering King teach us to do in suffering (vv. 4–5)?

   <u>He teaches us to look back to the past and see how God cared for his people throughout history.</u>

Jesus had this psalm on his mind while suffering on the cross (Matthew 27:46). He cried to God and yet trusted in him because of what he knew about God's faithfulness in the past.

In the midst of loneliness and darkness, pray that God would encourage us with his faithfulness to his people throughout history.

THURSDAY

Psalm 22:6-13 The King Is Mocked by People

1. How do people react to the suffering King (v. 7)?

   They mock him.

2. Whose sufferings does this psalm predict (v. 8; Matthew 27:43)?

   This psalm predicts many of Christ's sufferings.

We should not be surprised if we are mocked for our faith because even Christ was mocked for his faith.

Ask God for courage to endure mockery and other insults for our faith.

FRIDAY

Psalm 22:14-21 The King Is Attacked by Beasts

1. What do the people do with the King's clothes (v. 18)?

   They divide them and gamble for them.

2. What happened to Christ's clothes (Matthew 27:35)?

   They divided them and gambled for them.

Although this psalm was written a thousand years before Christ, God predicts the details of Christ's sufferings in it.

Ask God to increase faith in his word, which is so accurate in its predictions.

SATURDAY

Psalm 22:27–31 The King Is Victorious

1. What was the result of the King's sufferings (v. 27)?

   Many people will turn to him in praise and worship.

2. What was the result of Christ's sufferings (Acts 2:41)?

   Three thousand were added to the church in one day through Peter's preaching of Christ's sufferings.

God uses Christ's sufferings to turn many people to him.

Pray that tomorrow's preaching of Christ crucified will turn many souls to him.

SUNDAY

Read the most important verses that your pastor preached on today.

What did you learn about God?

What did you learn about sin?

What did you learn about Jesus?

What did you learn about living?

What is the biggest lesson from the sermon?

What does the sermon lead us to pray for?

EXPEDITION 18
MORE SONGS ABOUT THE COMING KING

OUR MAP

Now that we know who this suffering King is, let's put a spring in our step as we listen to two more beautiful songs that praise him for his glorious and everlasting kingdom.

 PRAYER POINTS

 SNAPSHOT VERSE
Psalm 72:17

MONDAY

Psalm 72:1-4 A Just King

 1. How will the King rule (v. 2)?

With righteousness and justice.

2. Who is this King especially concerned about (v. 4)?

The poor and needy.

 Christ is a unique King because his reign is perfectly righteous and he has special care for the poor and needy.

 Ask God to make us willing subjects under Christ's righteous reign and to come to him as poor and needy.

TUESDAY

Psalm 72:5–7 A Prosperous King

1. How long will the King's kingdom last (v. 5)?

   As long as the sun and moon.

2. How should this change our view of politics?

   We should remember that political leaders do not last, but Christ's kingdom does.

Christ's kingdom will last longer than any other kingdom on this earth.

Thank God that Christ's kingdom will last longer than any other kingdom in past or future history.

WEDNESDAY

Psalm 72:8–11 A King of Kings

1. How far will the King's kingdom extend (v. 8)?

   Over every piece of land and every ocean.

2. How much of your life is under Christ's rule?

   Discuss areas of life that we may resist asking Christ to rule over (e.g., technology, money, relationships).

Christ's kingdom is growing day by day, and he will eventually rule over everything.

Ask God to extend Christ's kingdom over all the world, including our little personal world.

THURSDAY

Psalm 72:12–15 A Merciful King

1. What will this King do for the poor and needy (vv. 12–13)?

   He will deliver, pity, and save them.

2. How can we get the King as our Savior?

   By admitting that we are poor and needy.

Christ loves to save the poor and needy.

Ask God to give us a poor and needy spirit so that Christ will deliver and save us.

FRIDAY

Psalm 72:16–20 A Blessed King

1. What will the nations call this King (v. 17)?

   Blessed, which means approved and happy.

2. What should we pray for (v. 19)?

   We should pray that the whole earth would be filled with Christ's glory.

The blessed name of Jesus is above every other name (Philippians 2:10).

Pray that God will help us to bow before Christ and confess him as Lord of all.

SATURDAY

Psalm 150 A Praised King

1. Who and what should praise the Lord (v. 6)?

   Everything.

2. How many times does this psalm command us to praise God?

   Twelve times.

Psalm 150 sums up what the other 149 psalms were all about—calling everything to praise God for everything.

Pray for a worshipful spirit that praises God at all times for all things.

SUNDAY

Read the most important verses that your pastor preached on today.

What did you learn about God?

_____

What did you learn about sin?

_____

What did you learn about Jesus?

_____

What did you learn about living?

_____

What is the biggest lesson from the sermon?

_____

What does the sermon lead us to pray for?

_____

EXPEDITION 19
A FORK IN THE ROAD

OUR MAP

Explorers often have to choose between two paths. One goes to the right and one goes to the left, but which one do we take? That's the choice we find in the book of Proverbs. Its main author, King Solomon, describes two roads—Wise Road and Foolish Road—and calls us to choose Wise Road and run from Foolish Road. We should listen to King Solomon because he was one of the wisest people ever (1 Kings 4:29–34).

 PRAYER POINTS

 SNAPSHOT VERSE
Proverbs 1:7

MONDAY

Proverbs 1:1–7 Wisdom Teaches

 1. Why did Solomon write Proverbs (v. 4)?

   To teach knowledge and discretion (wisdom) to young people.

2. What is the beginning of wisdom (v. 7)?

   The fear of the Lord.

 To fear the Lord is to respect the Lord more than anyone else and aim to please him in all things.

 Ask for the fear of the Lord that will start us on the path to true wisdom.

TUESDAY

Proverbs 1:8–14 Wisdom Appeals

 1. Whose instruction should you listen to (v. 8)?

Our father's and mother's instruction.

2. Who tempts you to reject your parents' instructions (vv. 10–11)?

Perhaps a friend, a neighbor, a fellow student, a celebrity.

 We live in a world full of temptation to depart from God and God-given authorities in our lives.

 Pray that God would keep us from temptation, make us deaf to it, or deliver us out of it.

WEDNESDAY

Proverbs 1:15–19 Wisdom Warns

 1. Why is it dangerous to walk in the foolish path of sinners (v. 16)?

Because they are running fast toward evil.

2. What are some of the dangerous traps God has already warned you about (v. 17)?

Dangerous friends, evil habits, and so forth.

 God knows the dangers that face us and has given us plenty of warning about how to avoid and escape their traps.

 Thank God for caring enough to warn us and for giving us parents caring enough to warn us about dangers we cannot see.

THURSDAY

Proverbs 1:20–23 Wisdom Calls

1. Who is Jesus Christ (1 Corinthians 1:24)?

   The power and wisdom of God.

2. What will Wisdom do if we listen and repent (v. 23)?

   Pour out his Spirit on us and teach us.

Because Jesus is the ultimate wisdom of God, let us turn to him and be taught by him.

Let us admit our ignorance and need of teaching, and turn to God's wisdom in Jesus to make us wise unto salvation.

FRIDAY

Proverbs 1:24–27 Wisdom Threatens

1. How do some people respond to God's wisdom (vv. 24–25)?

   They refuse it and don't listen to it.

2. What will Wisdom do if we do not listen (v. 26)?

   Wisdom will not help us when we are in the deepest trouble.

While Jesus calls us to him and offers us his wisdom, if we reject him, he will ultimately reject us.

Ask Jesus to be our teacher in the good times so that he will also help us in the bad times.

SATURDAY

Proverbs 1:28–33 Wisdom Secures

1. What are we doing if we reject God's wisdom (v. 29)?

   We are hating knowledge.

2. What will happen if we listen to God's wisdom (v. 33)?

   Our life will be safer and more peaceful.

Life is a choice between following God's wisdom or rejecting it (Matthew 7:13–14; 24–29).

Pray that God will help us to choose his wisdom, Jesus Christ, who is the way the truth and the life (John 14:6).

SUNDAY

Read the most important verses that your pastor preached on today.

What did you learn about God?

_____

What did you learn about sin?

_____

What did you learn about Jesus?

_____

What did you learn about living?

_____

What is the biggest lesson from the sermon?

_____

What does the sermon lead us to pray for?

_____

EXPEDITION 20
THE CHOICE

OUR MAP

Throughout Proverbs, King Solomon keeps reminding us of the choice between Wise Road and Foolish Road. Last week we looked at Solomon's longer descriptions of these two roads. This week we'll look at a number of snapshots that keep making us choose between Wise Road and Foolish Road.

 PRAYER POINTS

 SNAPSHOT VERSE
Proverbs 14:27

MONDAY

Proverbs 14:1–5 Foolish Lies

 1. What's the difference between a faithful witness and a false witness (v. 5)?

   <u>A false witness tells lies whereas a faithful witness tells the truth.</u>

   2. Who is the most faithful witness (Revelation 1:5)?

   <u>The Lord Jesus Christ.</u>

 Jesus Christ is our model of a faithful witness who tells us the truth about everything.

 Ask Jesus to tell you the truth and to make you a truth-teller.

TUESDAY

Proverbs 14:6–11 Foolish Laughter

1. How do fools react to sin (or to offering a sacrifice for sin) (v. 9)?

   They laugh at it.

2. What sins are you tempted to laugh at?

   Perhaps dirty jokes or bad language or sinful scenes in movies.

One of the most foolish things we can do is laugh at sin.

Ask God to help us treat sin with horror not humor.

WEDNESDAY

Proverbs 14:12–16 Foolish Confidence

1. What does a wise person do (v. 16)?

   They fear and turn away from evil.

2. What do foolish people do (v. 16)?

   They are self-confident, careless, and reckless in the face of sin.

Self-confidence is foolish and dangerous, but God-confidence is wise and safe.

Confess self-confidence, and ask God to give us God-confidence that will turn us away from sin.

THURSDAY

Proverbs 14:17–21 Wise Love

1. What will make you happy (blessed) (v. 21)?

   Being generous to the poor.

2. How can you show mercy to the poor?

   Give food for the body and food for the soul: bread for the mouth and God's word for the soul.

God finds happiness in showing us mercy by feeding us physically and spiritually, and he calls us to do the same to others.

Thank God for his mercy to us and pray for grace to do the same for others.

FRIDAY

Proverbs 14:22–29 Wise Fear

1. What is the fear of the Lord (v. 27)?

   A fountain of life.

2. Read verse 29 and ask yourself if you are wise or foolish according to this standard.

One of the greatest signs of wisdom is being patient and slow to anger.

Confess our foolish anger, and ask God to give us some of his wise patience.

SATURDAY

Proverbs 14:30–35 Wise Nation

1. What will make a nation great (v. 34)?

   Righteousness, which is obedience to God's law.

2. How can we improve our health (v. 30)?

   By cultivating a pure heart and turning from all sin, especially envy.

Obedience usually leads to a healthy body and a healthy nation.

Pray for life-giving and health-giving obedience for ourselves and our nation.

SUNDAY

Read the most important verses that your pastor preached on today.

What did you learn about God?

_____

What did you learn about sin?

_____

What did you learn about Jesus?

_____

What did you learn about living?

_____

What is the biggest lesson from the sermon?

_____

What does the sermon lead us to pray for?

_____

EXPEDITION 21
A DANGEROUS DETOUR

OUR MAP

In addition to Proverbs, Solomon wrote two other books—Ecclesiastes and Song of Solomon. Ecclesiastes tells us of a time when Solomon, despite being so wise, chose the path of sinful folly and ended up desperately unhappy. It's a book to warn us against following him down this road.

 PRAYER POINTS

 SNAPSHOT VERSE
Ecclesiastes 12:1

MONDAY

Ecclesiastes 1:12–18 Work without God

 1. How did Solomon describe himself (v. 12)?

The preacher and king of Israel.

2. What did Solomon see when he looked out over the world (v. 14)?

All is vanity (which means emptiness).

 Trying to find happiness in work will leave us feeling empty.

 Confess that we have tried to find satisfaction in work, and ask God to give us happiness in *his* works of providence and salvation.

TUESDAY

Ecclesiastes 2:1–6 Pleasure without God

1. What did Solomon try to make him happy (v. 1)?

Pleasure.

2. What will result if we try to find happiness in pleasure (v. 1)?

It will leave us feeling empty.

Pleasure-seeking does not satisfy.

Confess that we have tried to find happiness in seeking sinful pleasures, and ask God to give us happiness in him.

WEDNESDAY

Ecclesiastes 2:7–11 Possessions without God

1. What did Solomon try to make him happy (v. 7)?

Lots of possessions.

2. What was the result (v. 11)?

Solomon said the end result was emptiness.

Having lots of possessions does not satisfy.

Confess to God that we have tried to find happiness in material possessions and ask God to give us happiness in having God as our possession.

THURSDAY

Ecclesiastes 2:12–17 Education without God

1. What did Solomon try to make him happy (vv. 12–13)?

   Knowledge.

2. What was the result (v. 15)?

   Emptiness.

The pursuit of knowledge does not satisfy.

Confess to God that we have tried to find happiness in education and ask God to give us happiness in knowing him.

FRIDAY

Ecclesiastes 2:18–23 Wealth without God

1. What made Solomon sad (v. 18)?

   When he died he would have to leave all he worked for behind.

2. What will we end up with when we die (v. 22)?

   Nothing.

When we die, we can't take anything from this world with us.

Ask God to remind us that we will have to leave everything behind when we die.

SATURDAY

Ecclesiastes 2:24–26; 12:13–14 A Little with God

1. When Solomon put God at the center of his life, he could enjoy life's simplest pleasures and possessions (2:24, 26). How can you put God at the center of your life?

2. What did Solomon say after he had tried the wrong path (12:13)?

   The best way to live is to fear God (an Old Testament expression for faith in God) and obey him.

Putting God first and center in our lives produces the greatest happiness.

Pray that God will help us to trust him and obey him as the way to the happiest life.

SUNDAY

Read the most important verses that your pastor preached on today.

What did you learn about God?

What did you learn about sin?

What did you learn about Jesus?

What did you learn about living?

What is the biggest lesson from the sermon?

What does the sermon lead us to pray for?

EXPEDITION 22
LOVE SONGS

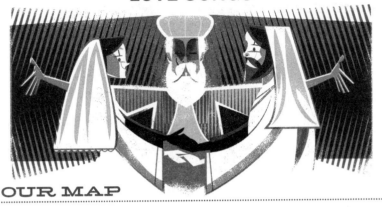

OUR MAP

I have many happy memories of family vacations when I was young. I can still remember the songs we used to sing in the car and where we were going when we sang them. Songs stick in our minds and help us to remember. Perhaps that's why God gave us the Song of Solomon or, as some Bibles title it, the "Song of Songs" (Song of Solomon 1:1). It's the best song ever because it describes the best love ever. It describes the love between a husband and a wife, but that man-woman love is also a picture or symbol of the love between God and Israel (Isaiah 54:5; Jeremiah 3:14) and between Christ and his church (Ephesians 5:23, 25). In this expedition we will focus on the love between Christ (the bridegroom) and his people (the bride).

 PRAYER POINTS

 SNAPSHOT VERSE
Song of Solomon 1:4

MONDAY

Song of Solomon 1:1–4 Love Is Passionate

 1. What does the bride want the bridegroom to do (v. 2)?

Kiss her, which means show her his love.

2. In what way is the bridegroom's love better than wine (v. 2)?

Unlike wine, his love can be enjoyed without hesitation or limitation.

 The believer wants to experience more and more of God's love through Christ.

 Thank God for marriage and for the joy God gives in it. Thank God for his love for his people and for the even greater joy in it.

TUESDAY

Song of Solomon 2:1-7 Love Is Public

1. What was the banner or flag over the shared feast (v. 4)?

   A banner, or flag, of love.

2. How does God make public his love for his people?

   By his many gifts to us, by his guidance of us, and above all by his public display of love in the cross of Christ.

God is not ashamed of his people and demonstrates it publicly in many ways.

Thank God for his unashamed love for sinners and his public proof of that in the cross.

WEDNESDAY

Song of Solomon 2:8-13 Love Is Lively

1. What does the bridegroom say to the bride (vv. 10, 13)?

   Arise, my love, and come away with me.

2. How does God ask us to rise up and come with him?

   By the preaching of the gospel, God calls us to himself.

When God calls us, we should come running to him.

Ask God for help to wake up, to hear his invitations, and to accept his welcome.

THURSDAY

Song of Solomon 2:14–17 Love Is Two-Way

1. What does the bride say about the bridegroom (v. 16)?

   My beloved is mine, and I am his.

2. Can you say these words about God? Is God your beloved possession? Are you God's beloved possession?

Assurance of God's love should lead us to express our love to him.

Ask God for assurance of his love and for help to express our love
to him.

FRIDAY

Song of Solomon 3:1–5 Love Is Longing

1. What did the bride do when she could not find her bridegroom
   (vv. 1–3)?

   She got up and searched for him.

2. What did the bride do when she found the bridegroom again (v. 4)?

   She held him and would not let him go.

If we love God, we will want to be close to him at all times.

Ask God to stay close to you and keep you close to him by giving you
permanent longing and desire for him.

SATURDAY

Song of Solomon 3:6–11 Love Is Joyful

1. Describe the bridegroom's heart on his wedding day (v. 11).

   He was glad.

2. What makes you happy when you think about being loved by God?

   There is no greater love than God's love and no greater evidence of it than Jesus dying for sinners like us.

Human marriage is one of the happiest blessings God can give us, but being married to God brings us even greater happiness.

Pray that God will give us a happy marriage, but even more that he would give us the greatest happiness of being married to him.

SUNDAY

Read the most important verses that your pastor preached on today.

What did you learn about God?

_____

What did you learn about sin?

_____

What did you learn about Jesus?

_____

What did you learn about living?

_____

What is the biggest lesson from the sermon?

_____

What does the sermon lead us to pray for?

_____

EXPEDITION 23
LOOKING INTO THE DISTANCE

OUR MAP

We're coming to the end of our exploration of the Old Testament. We've seen that God promised a special King who would deliver his people and defeat their enemies. Thus far we've been disappointed. That King has not yet come. But we mustn't give up hope of arriving at that destination. The prophets didn't. These were men whom God raised up and sent to his people to call them from their sins and to keep them hoping and looking for a great King and a great kingdom. Let's explore the Prophets together and discover some of their wonderful promises.

 PRAYER POINTS

 SNAPSHOT VERSE
Isaiah 9:6

MONDAY

Isaiah 7:10–16 A Godly King

 1. What does *Immanuel* mean (v. 14; Matthew 1:23)?

God with us.

2. How did Jesus fulfill this prophecy?

By becoming a man and living like us in this world.

 God's desire to be with us is proved in Jesus's birth and life.

 Praise God for wanting to be with us and for fulfilling this prophecy in Jesus becoming man.

TUESDAY

Isaiah 9:2-7 A Worldwide King

1. What are the names of this special child (v. 6)?

   Wonderful Counselor, Mighty God, Everlasting Father, Prince of Peace.

2. What is your favorite name for Jesus in this verse? Why?

Jesus lived up to all these names when he came to this world.

Praise God for the names of Jesus that reveal his beautiful character to us.

WEDNESDAY

Isaiah 11:1-5 A Wise King

1. What will rest upon this special king (v. 2)?

   The Spirit of the Lord.

2. How is the Spirit of the Lord described (v. 2)?

   The Spirit of wisdom, understanding, counsel, might, and knowledge.

The Lord Jesus was filled with the Holy Spirit for his great work.

Ask God that he would fill us with his Holy Spirit so that we may be wise.

THURSDAY

Isaiah 42:1–7 A Gentle King

1. How will the coming King deal with bruised reeds (v. 3)? (A "bruised reed" is a picture of broken people.)

   He will not break them.

2. What makes this King so different from other kings (v. 3)?

   He deals gently with the weak, the poor, and the wounded.

Jesus is the gentle King who fulfilled this prophecy (Matthew 12:20).

Ask King Jesus to rule over us with gentleness and kindness.

FRIDAY

Isaiah 53:1–6 A Suffering King

1. What will people do to this special King (v. 3)?

   Reject him and hide from him.

2. Why was this King wounded and bruised (v. 5)?

   For our sins.

Jesus died for the sins of sinners.

Ask Jesus to be our Savior from sin, to be our substitute dying in our place.

SATURDAY

Isaiah 53:7–12 A Victorious King

1. What kind of offering (or sacrifice) was Jesus's death (v. 10)?

   An offering for guilt (sin).

2. Isaiah 53:10–12 speak of the King's victory. What is the greatest evidence of Christ's victory?

   His resurrection from the dead (Matthew 28:5–7).

Although Jesus died the worst death, he was raised to life again and now reigns as the victorious King.

Praise God for Christ's victory and ask that his death would be our life.

SUNDAY

Read the most important verses that your pastor preached on today.

What did you learn about God?

_____

What did you learn about sin?

_____

What did you learn about Jesus?

_____

What did you learn about living?

_____

What is the biggest lesson from the sermon?

_____

What does the sermon lead us to pray for?

_____

EXPEDITION 24
THE GROWING EXCITEMENT

OUR MAP

As we finish our travels through the Old Testament, we learn even more about God's promised King. In addition to Isaiah, we hear from Jeremiah, Jonah, and Zechariah. They all increase our excitement and leave us on the edge of our seats, longing to see this long-awaited King. Who is he, and when will he come?

 PRAYER POINTS

 SNAPSHOT VERSE
Isaiah 61:1

MONDAY

Isaiah 60:1-5 The King Gives Light

1. How will the Gentiles (or nations) respond to this King (v. 3)?
They will come to his light.

2. What happens when we come to Christ's light (John 3:21)?
Our actions are exposed.

Christ's light attracts sinners but also exposes our sin.

Ask that God would draw us to Christ's light and show us our sins.

TUESDAY

Isaiah 61:1-6 The King Releases Prisoners

1. What will this King preach (v. 1)?

   Good news to the poor and liberty to the captives.

2. How does Jesus set us free (John 8:32, 36)?

   With the truth.

Jesus delivers people imprisoned by sin with the truth.

Ask Jesus to open the prison doors of sin and set us free with his truth.

WEDNESDAY

Jeremiah 31:31-34 The King Forgives Sin

1. What will God forgive and "forget" (v. 34)?

   Our sins.

2. What will happen if we have been forgiven many sins (Luke 7:47)?

   We will have much love for Christ.

Through Christ's death, God can forgive and forget our sins.

Ask God to forgive and forget our sins through Christ and to give us much love for him in return.

THURSDAY

Jonah 3:1-4 The King Warns Sinners

1. What was Jonah's warning (v. 4)?

   In forty days Nineveh will be destroyed.

2. What warnings has God given you, and what should you do with them?

   Ask your family to discuss times that God has given warnings through his providence, through preaching, or through parents.

In his love, God sends us messengers to warn us of God's coming judgment.

Ask God to help us to believe his warnings and to act upon them.

FRIDAY

Jonah 3:5-10 The King Gives Repentance

1. What did God do when the Ninevites repented (v. 10)?

   He decided not to destroy them.

2. What sins should you turn from to stop God's destruction?

Repentance turns from sin to God in order to stop God's destruction of us.

Ask God for true repentance that will turn us from sin to God and save us from destruction.

SATURDAY

Zechariah 12:9–13:1 The King Provides Cleansing

1. What does God open for sin (13:1)?

A fountain for cleansing.

2. Who is God's fountain to wash away our sin (1 John 1:9)?

Jesus cleanses us from every sin.

God's fountain, Jesus Christ, is an ever-flowing source of cleansing from sin.

Pray that God will cleanse us from our sin through Jesus Christ.

SUNDAY

Read the most important verses that your pastor preached on today.

What did you learn about God?

What did you learn about sin?

What did you learn about Jesus?

What did you learn about living?

What is the biggest lesson from the sermon?

What does the sermon lead us to pray for?

EXPEDITION 25
A STRANGE PLACE

OUR MAP

We've traveled many miles and many years in our journey through the Old Testament. We've explored many thick forests of biblical history. But we've also enjoyed many bright and beautiful views of a coming King. Now, after such a long wait, we're about to meet the King. God has given us four books about his life—the Gospels of Matthew, Mark, Luke, and John. Try to think of these four books as four different cameras that look at Jesus's life from four different angles. Over the next weeks we will be viewing the most important points in Jesus's life using each of these four cameras. We start with the birth of this King and the unusual palace he was born in.

 PRAYER POINTS

 SNAPSHOT VERSE
Matthew 1:21

MONDAY

Matthew 1:1–2; 15–17 The Baby's Parents

 1. Jesus is described as the son of . . . (v. 1).

The Son of David, the Son of Abraham.

2. Why does God give us Jesus's genealogy in Matthew 1?

To teach us that Jesus is the fulfillment of the Old Testament and that he was part of the human race.

 Jesus is the one to whom the whole Old Testament pointed. The Old Testament promise is kept in the New Testament.

 Thank God for keeping his promises, especially the promise of sending Jesus to save sinners.

TUESDAY

Matthew 1:18–21 The Baby's First Name

1. How did Mary become pregnant (v. 18, 20)?

   <u>By the Holy Spirit</u>

2. Why is Jesus's name precious to you (v. 21)?

   <u>It is precious because it tells us he came to save his people from their sins.</u>

Jesus's name means "God saves" and teaches us that God wants us to know him as the Savior of sinners.

Ask Jesus to live up to his name by saving us from our sins.

WEDNESDAY

Matthew 1:22–25 The Baby's Second Name

1. What name did the angel give to Mary and Joseph's son (v. 23)?

   <u>Immanuel.</u>

2. Why is Immanuel such a wonderful name (v. 23)?

   <u>Because it tells me that in Jesus, God is with us.</u>

Jesus proves that God loves to be with us.

Ask that we would love to be with God as much as he loves to be with us.

THURSDAY

Luke 2:1–7 The Baby's Crib

1. Where did Joseph go with Mary (v. 4)?

   To Bethlehem, the city of David.

2. What does Jesus's first bed tell us about him (v. 7)?

   The manger, or feeding trough, tells us that Jesus was willing to come down to the lowest level to save us.

No matter how low we are, Jesus will come down to our level to save us.

Thank God for Jesus being willing to come so low to save us.

FRIDAY

Luke 2:8–14 The Baby's Choir

1. What did the angel say to the shepherds (v. 10)?

   Fear not. I bring you good news of great joy to all people.

2. What should we sing about Jesus's birth (v. 14)?

   With the angels we should sing glory to God in the highest, and on earth peace, goodwill toward men.

Jesus's birth is a cause for joy and singing on earth.

Ask God to give us great joy and great songs over the birth of Jesus.

SATURDAY

Luke 2:15–20 The Baby's Impact

1. What did the shepherds do when they saw the baby (v. 17)?

   They told everyone about it.

2. Who can you tell about Jesus this coming week (v. 20)?

   Talk about ways to share the good news of Jesus with others.

We should tell everyone about Jesus and praise God for Jesus.

Pray that God would help us tell others about Jesus and to praise him for Jesus.

SUNDAY

Read the most important verses that your pastor preached on today.

What did you learn about God?

_____

What did you learn about sin?

_____

What did you learn about Jesus?

_____

What did you learn about living?

_____

What is the biggest lesson from the sermon?

_____

What does the sermon lead us to pray for?

_____

EXPEDITION 26
A TEMPLE AND A RIVER

OUR MAP

We would love to know more about Jesus's life as a boy and as a young man. However, the Bible tells us about only one event in his childhood, the time he visited the temple when he was twelve years old. The next time we hear of him, he is thirty years old and is being baptized by John the Baptist in the River Jordan just before beginning his public ministry. Let's look at both of these events, starting with his visit to the temple.

 PRAYER POINTS

 SNAPSHOT VERSE
Luke 2:52

_____

_____

MONDAY

Luke 2:39–42 Jesus Grows Up

 1. Describe Jesus's growth (v. 40).

He grew in size and in wisdom.

2. How do we fill up with wisdom (v. 40)?

By reading God's word and seeking God's grace.

 If we grow in wisdom by reading God's word, his grace, or his favor, will be upon us.

 Ask God to make us wise through his word.

TUESDAY

Luke 2:43–47 Jesus Teaches the Teachers

1. How did the people in the temple react to Jesus (v. 47)?

   They were amazed at his understanding and his answers.

2. What is the best way to learn (v. 46)?

   Like Jesus did, by listening and asking questions.

The best way to learn, as Jesus showed, is by listening and by asking questions about the Bible.

Ask God for help to learn like Jesus by listening to and asking questions about the Bible.

WEDNESDAY

Luke 2:48–52 Jesus Submits to His parents

1. What did Mary do with all that she saw Jesus do (v. 51)?

   She treasured all these things in her heart.

2. What does Jesus's relationship to his parents teach us (v. 51)?

   Like Jesus, we should submit to our parents, which means we should humbly obey them.

We can grow in wisdom like Jesus by obeying our parents like Jesus did.

Confess that there are times when we have not obeyed our parents like Jesus did.

THURSDAY

Mark 1:1–8 John the Baptist Announces Jesus

1. What did John the Baptist preach (v. 4)?

   <u>A baptism of repentance for the forgiveness of sins.</u>

2. What do we need in order to repent and to receive the forgiveness of sins (v. 8)?

   <u>We need Jesus to give us the Holy Spirit.</u>

Just as water washes dirt away, so the Holy Spirit washes sin away.

Pray for the Holy Spirit to wash away our sin.

FRIDAY

Mark 1:9–13 Jesus Is Baptized in the Jordan

1. What did the voice from heaven say to Jesus (v. 11)?

   <u>God told Jesus that he loved him and was pleased with him.</u>

2. Satan tempted Jesus (v. 13). How does Satan tempt you?

Contrast the love of God with the hatred of Satan and ask yourself whose voice you really want to follow.

Pray for more of God's love in our lives and to be protected from Satan's hatred.

SATURDAY

Mark 1:14–18 Jesus Begins to preach

1. What was Jesus's first sermon (v. 15)?

   <u>The time is fulfilled, and the kingdom of God is at hand. Repent and believe the gospel.</u>

2. What does it mean to become a fisher of men (v. 17)?

   <u>It means that people are swimming in sin, and Jesus wants his followers to help rescue them.</u>

We cannot follow Jesus and help save other people from their sins until we have repented of our sins and believed the gospel.

Pray for repentance and faith in Jesus so that we can follow him.

SUNDAY

Read the most important verses that your pastor preached on today.

What did you learn about God?

What did you learn about sin?

What did you learn about Jesus?

What did you learn about living?

What is the biggest lesson from the sermon?

What does the sermon lead us to pray for?

EXPEDITION 27
A CHURCH ON A MOUNTAIN

OUR MAP

Jesus's most famous sermon is his Sermon on the Mount. Let's stop on that hillside for a while and listen to his wonderful preaching. We begin with the Beatitudes, which describe the blessed character of the citizens in Christ's kingdom. After that we will look at the conduct of these citizens, how they are to live in this world.

 PRAYER POINTS

 SNAPSHOT VERSE
Matthew 5:3

MONDAY

Matthew 5:1–6 Kingdom Character (1)

 1. What is given to the poor in spirit (v. 3)?

The kingdom of heaven.

2. What should we mourn over (v. 4)?

We should be sad for our sins.

 God comforts us when we are sad about our sins by assuring us of his forgiveness through Jesus Christ.

 Confess our sins with sadness and be comforted by God's forgiveness.

TUESDAY

Matthew 5:7–12 Kingdom Character (2)

1. Who will see God (v. 8)?

   The pure in heart.

2. How do you know if you are a child of God (v. 9)?

   One evidence is that we will be a peacemaker.

Jesus, the Son of God, has the purest heart and is the greatest peacemaker.

Ask God to make us like Jesus, pure in heart and peacemaking.

WEDNESDAY

Matthew 5:13–16 Kingdom Light

1. What are Christians called (v. 14)?

   The light of the world.

2. How do we let our light shine in the world (vv. 15–16)?

   By not hiding that we are Christians and by doing good works to others.

God has called Christians to shine in the darkness of this world.

Ask God for courage to be a public witness to Christ and to do good to others.

THURSDAY

Matthew 5:17–20 Kingdom Fulfillment

1. What did Jesus come to do with the Law and the Prophets (v. 17)?

   To fulfill them.

2. What kind of righteousness do we need to get to heaven (v. 20)?

   A righteousness that exceeds that of the scribes and Pharisees.

Although we cannot make a better righteousness than the scribes and Pharisees, Jesus did and offers it to us (2 Corinthians 5:21).

Ask God to give us the perfect righteousness of Christ that we may go to heaven.

FRIDAY

Matthew 5:21–26 Kingdom Judgment

1. What puts us in danger of God's judgment (v. 22)?

   Being angry without a good reason.

2. What are we to do if we come to worship God when someone is angry with us (vv. 23–24)?

   We are to seek him out and try and reconcile with him first.

Sinful anger is dangerous and therefore must be avoided or dealt with in God's way.

Ask God to take away sinful anger from our hearts and to renew friendship with those who may be angry with us.

SATURDAY

Matthew 5:27–32 Kingdom Marriage

1. What does Jesus forbid (v. 28)?

   He forbids having sinful thoughts and desires, not just sinful actions.

2. What does Jesus mean by plucking out our eye if it causes us to sin (v. 29)?

   He means that we are to do all that we need to do to stop our eyes from sinning.

God requires not only holy actions, but holy hearts and minds.

Pray that God will give us pure hearts and minds so that we will also have pure eyes.

SUNDAY

Read the most important verses that your pastor preached on today.

What did you learn about God?

What did you learn about sin?

What did you learn about Jesus?

What did you learn about living?

What is the biggest lesson from the sermon?

What does the sermon lead us to pray for?

EXPEDITION 28
ENEMIES

OUR MAP

Sometimes explorers can encounter enemies in their travels. But in this part of Jesus's sermon, we'll discover that Jesus has an unusual way of dealing with enemies.

 PRAYER POINTS

 SNAPSHOT VERSE
Matthew 5:48

MONDAY

Matthew 5:33–37 Kingdom Words

---

 1. What does God say about "yes" and "no" (v. 37)?

We are to let our yes be yes and our no be no.

2. What does this mean?

It means that our words are to be totally truthful at all times.

 It is the evil devil who loves lies and wants us to lie (v. 37).

 Pray that God will make us like Jesus, who was totally truthful and reliable.

TUESDAY

Matthew 5:38–42 Kingdom Kindness

1. What are we to do if someone wants to borrow something (v. 42)?

   We are to give what they ask for.

2. Why is it so hard to obey these commands?

   Because our hearts are not like Jesus.

On a personal level, we are to be kind and helpful to those who are not kind and helpful to us because that's what Jesus did.

Ask God to give us the heart of Jesus that will be kind and helpful even to those who hate us.

WEDNESDAY

Matthew 5:43–48 Kingdom Enemies

1. What should we do to our personal enemies (v. 44)?

   Love them, bless them, do good to them, and pray for them.

2. How can you obey this verse with your greatest enemy?

   Discuss with your family how to practice verse 44 within their own specific situations.

If we love our enemies as God does, we prove that we are his children (v. 45).

Praise God for loving enemies like us, confess our lack of love to our enemies, and pray for grace to be more God-like in our dealings with our enemies.

THURSDAY

Matthew 6:1–4 Kingdom Giving

1. Who is to see our religious and charitable activities (alms) (v. 4)?

   Our Father in heaven.

2. What will God do if we secretly give money to the church or to someone in need (v. 4)?

   He will reward us.

We are to give to God and do good to others without trying to get others to see what we are doing.

Ask God for help to do good things for his eyes only without telling or showing others on social media or any other ways.

FRIDAY

Matthew 6:5–8 Kingdom Religion

1. What does God know before we pray (v. 8)?

   He knows what we need.

2. What are your needs today?

   Discuss specific needs of different family members.

When we pray, we pray to someone who already knows all about us and yet wants to hear us tell him ourselves.

Let us tell God our needs, knowing that he knows already and yet still enjoys hearing us tell him.

SATURDAY

Matthew 6:9–15 Kingdom Prayer

 1. What will happen if we do not forgive others (v. 15)?

God will not forgive us our sins.

2. Who do you find hardest to forgive and why?

Talk about intersibling challenges especially.

 God will forgive us our sins only insofar as we forgive others their sins.

 Pray for our sins to be forgiven in such a way that we find it easy to forgive others' sins.

SUNDAY

Read the most important verses that your pastor preached on today.

 What did you learn about God?

What did you learn about sin?

What did you learn about Jesus?

What did you learn about living?

What is the biggest lesson from the sermon?

What does the sermon lead us to pray for?

EXPEDITION 29
HEAVENLY TREASURE

OUR MAP

The Sermon on the Mount is a long sermon, isn't it? But because Jesus was preaching it, I'm sure it wasn't boring. In this part he teaches us about money and worry. He also tells us what we should seek first in our travels.

 PRAYER POINTS

 SNAPSHOT VERSE
Matthew 6:33

MONDAY

Matthew 6:16–18 Kingdom Words

 1. Where is fasting to take place (v. 18)?

In secret.

2. Fasting was a way of freeing time for God. What can we give up today in order to free up time for God?

Technology, video games, social media, sports, and so on.

 God sometimes calls us to fast from things that take up our time in order to give him more time.

 Pray that God will help us to sacrifice some less important things in order to get more time with him.

TUESDAY

Matthew 6:19–21 Kingdom Treasure

1. Where is our treasure to be (vv. 19–20)?

Not on earth but in heaven.

2. Where will our hearts be (v. 21)?

Our hearts will be where our treasure is.

Our hearts and minds will focus on what we count most valuable.

Ask God to help us value spiritual and heavenly things more than physical and earthly things so that our hearts and minds will be more holy than worldly.

WEDNESDAY

Matthew 6:22–24 Kingdom Light

1. What is the lamp or light of the body (v. 22)?

The eye.

2. What is impossible to do (v. 24)?

It is impossible to serve two masters.

If we let the light of God's truth into our eyes, we will find it easier to serve him as our Master.

Ask God to open our eyes to his truth and to serve him as our Master.

THURSDAY

Matthew 6:25–30 Kingdom Peace

1. Where does Jesus point us to help us stop worrying (v. 26)?

   The little birds.

2. Why do the birds help us to stop worrying (v. 26)?

   They help us to see that if God provides for these little creatures, he will also provide for his beloved children.

God gives us images in nature to drive out anxiety.

Ask God to help us use the images he has placed in nature to calm our anxiety and give us peace.

FRIDAY

Matthew 6:31–34 Kingdom First

1. What are we to seek first (v. 33)?

   The kingdom of God and his righteousness.

2. What things can we often put ahead of God and his kingdom?

   Sports, studies, friends, phones, and so on.

King Jesus demands first place in our lives.

Confess the many times we have put Jesus second or third or even worse, and pray for help to put him first and keep him first.

SATURDAY

Matthew 7:1–6 **Kingdom Judgment**

1. What should we do first (v. 5)?

   Take the plank or log out of our own eye.

2. What should we do second (v. 5)?

   Take the speck of dust out of our brother's eye.

We tend to make our own faults smaller and others' faults bigger.

Pray that God would reverse our view of sin so that we see our own sin as worse than anyone else's, so that we deal with our sin first and most.

SUNDAY

Read the most important verses that your pastor preached on today.

What did you learn about God?

_____

What did you learn about sin?

_____

What did you learn about Jesus?

_____

What did you learn about living?

_____

What is the biggest lesson from the sermon?

_____

What does the sermon lead us to pray for?

_____

EXPEDITION 30
TWO HOUSES

OUR MAP

One of the reasons the Sermon on the Mount is so interesting and enjoyable is that Jesus uses so many pictures, images, and stories to illustrate his teaching. As he finishes his sermon, he uses the pictures of door-knocking, road travel, fruit trees, and house-building. He uses these pictures to call us to enter his kingdom and live a kingdom life.

 PRAYER POINTS

 SNAPSHOT VERSE
Matthew 7:24, 26.

Two verses this week, but they are similar in many ways.

MONDAY

Matthew 7:7–12 Knocking on the Kingdom's Door

1. What are we to do in prayer (v. 7)?

   Ask, seek, and knock.

2. What does our heavenly Father give (v. 11)?

   He gives good things to those who ask for them.

Jesus encourages us to pray because of our heavenly Father's goodness and grace.

Praise our heavenly Father for his good gifts, which he is more than willing to give to those who ask for them.

TUESDAY

Matthew 7:13-14 Traveling the Kingdom's Road

1. Describe the narrow way (v. 14).

   It leads to life but not many are on it.

2. How do we enter the narrow gate (v. 14)?

   By turning from the broad way with repentance and believing in Jesus, who said he was the way, the truth, and the life (John 14:6).

God calls us from the broad and popular road that leads to destruction, and calls us to enter the narrow and sometimes lonely road that leads to life.

Pray that God would save us all, and many others, from the broad road, and instead put us on the narrow path to life.

WEDNESDAY

Matthew 7:15-20 Bearing Kingdom Fruit

1. How do we know if a tree is good or bad (v. 20)?

   By the kind of fruit it produces, whether good or bad.

2. What kind of fruit do you see in your life, and what does it tell you about your life?

   Read Galatians 5:19-23 to help you identify different fruits.

God must make us good trees if we are to produce good fruit.

Ask God to make us into good trees that produce good fruit.

THURSDAY

Matthew 7:21–23 Doing the Kingdom's Will

1. Who will enter the kingdom of heaven (v. 21)?

   Those who do God's will.

2. What kind of people will hear Jesus's words "I never knew you" (v. 23).

   People who, though they talked much about religion, practiced lawlessness.

It's not enough to *talk* a lot about God's will. We must *do* it if we are to be saved.

Pray that God would deliver us from being mere talkers, and instead make us doers of his word.

FRIDAY

Matthew 7:24–27 Building on Kingdom Rock

1. Describe what happened to the two houses in the storm (vv. 25, 27).

   The house on the rock did not fall but the house on the sand fell down.

2. What is the difference between the wise and foolish person (vv. 24, 26)?

   The wise man hears God's word and does it, but the foolish man hears it and does not do it.

Jesus sets before us two very different people living two very different lives with two very different ends.

Ask God that Christ's clear words would give us clarity about our own spiritual state.

SATURDAY

Matthew 7:28–29 Responding to Kingdom Teaching

1. How did people respond to Jesus's sermon (v. 28)?

   They were astonished, especially because he taught with such authority.

2. What has astonished you about Christ's teaching?

   Ask your family what has most amazed them about Christ's Sermon on the Mount.

Christ's teaching is so clear and powerful that it should astonish us.

Thank God if Christ's teaching has left you astonished.

SUNDAY

Read the most important verses that your pastor preached on today.

What did you learn about God?

What did you learn about sin?

What did you learn about Jesus?

What did you learn about living?

What is the biggest lesson from the sermon?

What does the sermon lead us to pray for?

EXPEDITION 31
A SAD WEDDING AND A DIRTY TEMPLE

OUR MAP

We've just heard Jesus's first sermon. Now let's see Jesus's first miracle, followed by his cleansing of the temple. Then let's skip ahead to the book of 1 Peter to see what he teaches about the temple.

 PRAYER POINTS

 SNAPSHOT VERSE
John 2:16

MONDAY

John 2:1–5 A Sad Wedding

 1. Where did Jesus and his disciples go (v. 2)?

A wedding in Cana.

2. What did Jesus's mother say to the servants (v. 5)?

Do whatever Jesus tells you to do.

 Jesus's attendance at a wedding shows us his interest in everyday life and his joy in supporting marriage.

 Pray for Christ's blessing on marriage, especially the marriages of those close to us.

TUESDAY

John 2:6–11 A Happy Wedding

1. What did Jesus show or manifest at the wedding (v. 11)?

   His miracle of turning water into wine showed his glory.

2. What should we do when we read about Christ's glorious miracles (v. 11)?

   We should put our trust in Jesus because his miracles prove that he was God.

Jesus's miracles were designed to show his glory and create faith.

Ask Jesus to help you believe in him as you read about his glorious miracles.

WEDNESDAY

John 2:13–17 A Dirty Temple

1. Why was Jesus angry (v. 16)?

   Because people had turned the temple of God into a business.

2. What does Jesus's example here teach us about God's house (v. 17)?

   We are to have a zeal or passion for the purity of God's house.

Christ's example calls us to the reformation of the church so that it pleases God.

Thank God for the church and pray for passion to seek its purity.

THURSDAY

John 2:18-22 A New Temple

1. What temple was Jesus speaking about (v. 21)?

   The temple of his body.

2. How was Christ's prediction that he would raise up the destroyed temple fulfilled (v. 22)?

   By the resurrection of his body.

The resurrection is the miracle that showed Christ's glory in the greatest way and should lead to the greatest faith (v. 22).

Thank God for the resurrection and ask God for greater faith to result from it.

FRIDAY

1 Peter 2:1-6 A Living Temple

1. What kind of stone is Christ (v. 4)?

   A living stone, a rejected stone, a chosen and precious stone.

2. Who are the stones in Jesus's new temple (v. 5)?

   Jesus builds his temple out of believers.

The church is made not of dead stones but of living stones, of believers who find life in Christ.

Ask God to build his church by adding new believers to the foundation stone of Jesus Christ.

SATURDAY

1 Peter 2:7–10 A Preaching Temple

1. What does this new temple do (v. 9)?

   It proclaims the praises of the God who has called sinners out of darkness into his marvelous light.

2. How can you proclaim God's praises in your daily life?

   Talk about opportunities to speak about the Lord in daily life and situations.

God makes all his people preachers of his darkness-dispelling light.

Ask that God would make us better preachers of his darkness-defeating light.

SUNDAY

Read the most important verses that your pastor preached on today.

What did you learn about God?

_____

What did you learn about sin?

_____

What did you learn about Jesus?

_____

What did you learn about living?

_____

What is the biggest lesson from the sermon?

_____

What does the sermon lead us to pray for?

_____

EXPEDITION 32
A NIGHTTIME VISITOR

OUR MAP

We learn so much about Jesus from his sermons and his miracles. But we also learn a lot from listening to his conversations with others who needed to hear the gospel. This week we listen in on a conversation between Jesus and Nicodemus, an important religious leader. He visited Jesus in the middle of the night because he was afraid to be seen talking to Jesus.

 PRAYER POINTS

 SNAPSHOT VERSE
John 3:16

_____

_____

MONDAY

John 3:1-4 A New Birth

1. What must happen if we want to see the kingdom of God (v. 3)?
   We must be born again.

2. What does it mean to be born again (v. 4)?
   It is to get new spiritual life from God.

We are born into this world as sinners and need to be born again if we are to enter heaven.

Ask God for the new birth for ourselves and others.

TUESDAY

John 3:5–10 A Powerful Wind

1. What can flesh produce, and what can the Spirit produce (v. 6)?

   The flesh can produce only flesh but the Spirit can produce spirit.

2. How is the wind a good way to illustrate the new birth (v. 8)?

   It is a good way to illustrate the new birth because God is completely sovereign over the wind and the new birth. He alone can give both.

Only God's Spirit—not human effort—can produce spiritual birth (John 1:13).

Admit that we cannot make ourselves to be born again and pray for the Holy Spirit to blow new life into many souls, including our own.

WEDNESDAY

John 3:11–15 A Saving Snake

1. What did Moses lift up in the wilderness (v. 14; Numbers 21:7–9)?

   He lifted up a serpent on a pole.

2. What is the lesson from this story of the serpent on the pole (vv. 14–15)?

   Just as poisoned people looked to the serpent and were saved, so we will be saved if we look to the cross where Christ died for sin.

Sin is a poison, and the antidote is to look in faith to the cross where Christ died for sin.

Pray for Christ to be lifted up in the preaching of his word so that many look and are saved from the deadly poison of sin.

THURSDAY

John 3:16–21 A Sending Love

1. What made God send Jesus into the world (v. 16)?

   His love.

2. What was God's aim in sending Jesus into the world (v. 17)?

   To save sinners like us.

God's love sent Jesus to save a dying world.

Thank God for the great gift of his Son, the Lord Jesus, and pray for faith in him that we may not be condemned but saved.

FRIDAY

John 3:25–30 A Beautiful Humility

1. What was John the Baptist's desire (v. 30)?

   He wanted Jesus to increase and himself to decrease.

2. How can you make Jesus increase and yourself decrease?

   We can make Jesus increase by talking about him more than ourselves, and talking about ourselves much less.

Our life mission is the increase of Jesus.

Ask for a willingness to be less if Jesus could be more.

SATURDAY

John 3:31–36 A Clear Choice

1. What happens to all who believe in the Son of God (v. 36)?

   They have everlasting life.

2. What happens to those who do not believe on the Son of God (v. 36)?

   They will not see life but instead the wrath of God rests on them.

Jesus has made very clear that there are only two classes of people, believers and unbelievers, with two very different ends, life or his anger.

Pray that we and others will believe and have life, and that those who are presently under God's anger would enter into his love by faith.

SUNDAY

Read the most important verses that your pastor preached on today.

What did you learn about God?

What did you learn about sin?

What did you learn about Jesus?

What did you learn about living?

What is the biggest lesson from the sermon?

What does the sermon lead us to pray for?

EXPEDITION 33
WATER IN THE DESERT

OUR MAP

In our last expedition we listened to Jesus talking to Nicodemus, a very religious man. In this expedition, we're going to travel to a well in a desert to listen to his conversation with a Samaritan woman, a very sinful woman.

 PRAYER POINTS

 SNAPSHOT VERSE
John 4:14

MONDAY

John 4:5–8 Jesus Asks for a Drink

1. Why did Jesus sit by the well (v. 6)?

   <u>He was tired and thirsty.</u>

2. What does this fatigue and thirst tell us about Jesus?

   <u>It tells us that he was human like we are.</u>

Jesus got tired, thirsty, and hungry, like we do.

Praise God for the real humanity of Jesus and for the way that it helps both him to sympathize with us and us to draw near to him, as someone who experienced and understands our lives.

TUESDAY

John 4:9–14 Jesus Offers a Drink

1. What did Jesus offer the Samaritan woman (v. 10)?

   Living water.

2. What will happen to those who drink of Jesus's living water (v. 14)?

   They will never thirst because they will have a spring of refreshment inside them.

When we receive Jesus into our lives by faith, he is a life-giving and refreshing spring within us.

Ask Jesus for his life-giving water, his refreshing presence in our life.

WEDNESDAY

John 4:15–21 Jesus Creates Thirst

1. How many husbands had the woman had (v. 18)?

   Five.

2. Why did the Samaritan woman call Jesus a prophet (v. 19)?

   Because she knew that he knew all about her life.

Jesus knows all about us—all our past, present, and future.

Confess our sins to Jesus and ask him to show us sins that we have forgotten or that we don't even know we have committed.

THURSDAY

John 4:22–27 Jesus Wants Worshipers

 1. What does the Father seek (v. 23)?

The Father seeks worshipers to worship him.

2. What does it mean to worship God in spirit and in truth (v. 24)?

It means to worship him with the heart and according to his word.

 God seeks worshipers among the most unlikely of people and calls us to worship him with the heart.

 Praise God if he has sought us out and made us true worshipers, and ask that God will add many more surprising people to his worshipers.

FRIDAY

John 4:28–34 Jesus Saves a Sinner

 1. What did the woman do (v. 29)?

She invited other Samaritans to come and see Jesus.

2. What was Jesus's food (v. 34)?

His food was to do God's will and finish his work.

 Jesus was deeply satisfied by seeing the Samaritan woman saved and evangelizing others.

 Ask God to give us satisfaction in his service and to find our deepest joy in seeing souls saved and serving.

SATURDAY

John 4:39–42 **Jesus Saves Many Sinners**

1. What was the result of the Samaritan woman's witness (v. 39)?

   <u>Many of the Samaritans believed in Jesus.</u>

2. How did the Samaritans describe Jesus (v. 42)?

   <u>The Christ, the Savior of the world.</u>

Jesus came to save all kinds of people from all over the world.

Pray that we will follow the Samaritan woman's example and believe in Jesus and tell others about Jesus.

SUNDAY

Read the most important verses that your pastor preached on today.

What did you learn about God?

_____

What did you learn about sin?

_____

What did you learn about Jesus?

_____

What did you learn about living?

_____

What is the biggest lesson from the sermon?

_____

What does the sermon lead us to pray for?

_____

EXPEDITION 34
WONDERS OF THE WORLD

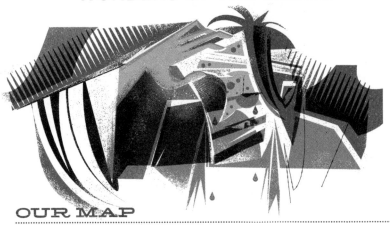

OUR MAP

Just as ancient explorers discovered the Seven Wonders of the Ancient World, this week's expedition will discover some of Jesus's wonders. We will see people wowed by his wonderful healings, and then the disciples wowed by his wonderful glory.

 PRAYER POINTS

 SNAPSHOT VERSE
Mark 2:5

_____

_____

MONDAY

Mark 1:23–28 Jesus Amazes with His Power

 1. What did the demon call Jesus (v. 24)?

The Holy One of God.

2. Why were the people amazed (v. 27)?

Because Jesus could command demons to leave a person.

 Only the Holy One of God can defeat the most unholy of spirits.

 Ask our holy God to defeat all unholy spirits that are destroying lives even today.

TUESDAY

Mark 1:29–35 **Jesus Heals Multitudes**

1. What did Jesus do first thing in the morning (v. 35)?

   He went to pray alone.

2. What can you learn from Jesus about where and when to pray?

   Discuss the best times, places, and ways to pray in our personal lives.

If Jesus needed to get up early and have time to pray alone with God, how much more do we!

Lord, teach us to pray!

WEDNESDAY

Mark 1:40–45 **Jesus Cleanses a Leper**

1. What did Jesus say to the leper (v. 41)?

   I am willing, be clean.

2. How is leprosy a picture of sin?

   Because, like leprosy, sin is infectious, it makes us unclean, it is painful, and it will ultimately kill us if we don't get cured and cleansed.

Sin is like a disease that eats away at us and eventually destroys us.

Join the leper in saying to God that if he is willing, he can make us clean of our sin.

THURSDAY

Mark 2:1–5 Jesus Forgives the Guilty

1. What did Jesus say to the lame man (v. 5)?

   He said his sins were forgiven.

2. How do you receive Christ's forgiveness for your sins?

   By confessing your sins and asking for his forgiveness.

Jesus can forgive us of every sin, even the ones that leave us weak and paralyzed.

Let us confess our sins to Jesus and ask for his free and full forgiveness.

FRIDAY

Mark 2:6–12 Jesus Enables the Disabled

1. What does Jesus have power to do (v. 10)?

   To forgive sins.

2. How does Jesus prove his power to forgive sins (vv. 10–11)?

   By commanding the lame man to walk.

Only Jesus has the authority and power to forgive sins.

Praise God for Jesus and for his commanding power to forgive sins.

SATURDAY

Mark 9:2–8 Jesus Shines Like the Sun

1. What did Jesus look like on the mountain (v. 3)?

   Very white and bright.

2. What did the voice from heaven say (v. 7)?

   This is my beloved Son. Hear him!

God the Father loves his Son, and he loves when we listen to him.

Ask God for greater love for Jesus and for better listening to Jesus.

SUNDAY

Read the most important verses that your pastor preached on today.

What did you learn about God?

_____

What did you learn about sin?

_____

What did you learn about Jesus?

_____

What did you learn about living?

_____

What is the biggest lesson from the sermon?

_____

What does the sermon lead us to pray for?

_____

EXPEDITION 35
LOST AND FOUND

OUR MAP

If we were to follow the Bible perfectly, we would never go astray and get lost. But when we disobey or forget the Bible and end up lost, what then? Is there any hope for us? Can we ever get back on track? To find out, we're going to explore three of Jesus's parables. Parables are earthly stories with heavenly meanings. The three parables in this week's expedition will take us to a mountainside, a house, and a pigpen in a faraway country.

 PRAYER POINTS

 SNAPSHOT VERSE
Luke 15:10

MONDAY

Luke 15:1–7 The Lost Sheep

 1. What does the shepherd do when one of his sheep gets lost (v. 4)?

He leaves the safe sheep and goes to find the lost one.

2. What does the shepherd's reaction tell us about Jesus (vv. 5–7)?

It tells us that he enjoys finding lost sinners and bringing them to safety.

 Jesus loves to find lost sheep and bring them back to God.

 Ask the good Shepherd to find you and bring you back to God with joy.

TUESDAY

Luke 15:8-10 The Lost Coin

1. What did the lady say to her neighbors when she found the lost coin (v. 9)?

   <u>Rejoice with me, for I have found the coin that I had lost.</u>

2. What makes heaven happy (v. 10)?

   <u>Sinners that repent make heaven happy.</u>

Although repentance means being sad and sorry about our sins, repentance makes heaven rejoice.

Ask for the kind of repentance that makes us sad but heaven happy.

WEDNESDAY

Luke 15:11-16 The Lost Son

1. What did the Prodigal Son do in the faraway country (v. 13)?

   <u>He wasted all of his money.</u>

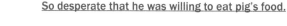

2. How desperate did he get (v. 16)?

   <u>So desperate that he was willing to eat pig's food.</u>

Sin drives us far away from God and makes us desperate.

Ask God to stop us from ever becoming a prodigal son or daughter.

THURSDAY

Luke 15:17–21 A Father Finds His Son

1. How did the Prodigal's father react when he saw him (v. 20)?

   He saw him from far away, ran to him, and kissed him.

2. What did the Prodigal say to his father (v. 21)?

   I have sinned, and I'm not worthy to be called your son anymore.

God loves to welcome humble sinners back into his love.

Ask that God would draw prodigals back to himself and thank God that he receives sinners like the Prodigal's father did.

FRIDAY

Luke 15:22–27 A Father Rejoices Over His Son

1. What did the father order to be put on his son (v. 22)?

   The best robe, a ring, and shoes.

2. What was the father's message to his servants (vv. 23–24)?

   Let's celebrate because my son was dead but now is alive; he was lost and now is found.

When God welcomes prodigals back, he does so with a joyful heart.

Praise God that he is so welcoming to sinners and gives us so many blessings in his salvation.

SATURDAY

Luke 15:28–32 A Father Rebukes His Son

1. How did the older brother react (v. 28)?

He was angry that his father was giving such a welcome to his younger brother.

2. Who was the older brother like (v. 2)?

He was like the proud and self-righteous Pharisees.

If we get angry over terrible sinners being saved, we have never been saved ourselves.

Pray to be delivered from a spirit of self-righteousness and for a godly spirit of joy over sinners repenting.

SUNDAY

Read the most important verses that your pastor preached on today.

What did you learn about God?

What did you learn about sin?

What did you learn about Jesus?

What did you learn about living?

What is the biggest lesson from the sermon?

What does the sermon lead us to pray for?

EXPEDITION 36
A SHEPHERD, A SERVANT,
A VINEDRESSER, AND A BUILDER

OUR MAP

Jesus loved to teach using pictures. This week we'll explore four pictures he used to describe himself: a shepherd to guide us, a servant to care for us, a builder to prepare a home for us, and a vine that makes us fruitful.

 PRAYER POINTS

 SNAPSHOT VERSE
John 14:6

MONDAY

John 10:1-6 The Shepherd Calls His Sheep

1. Why do sheep follow their shepherd (v. 4)?

   They know his voice.

2. How do we hear Christ's voice?

   He speaks to us through the Bible.

 Christ's sheep follow his voice as they hear it in the Bible.

 Ask for help to recognize and follow Christ's voice in the Bible.

TUESDAY

John 10:7–13 The Shepherd Saves His Sheep

1. Why did Jesus come to the world (v. 10)?

   To give abundant life.

2. What does the good shepherd do (v. 11)?

   He gives his life for the sheep.

Jesus gives life *to* his sheep by giving his life *for* his sheep.

Pray that we will receive life from Christ by faith in his sacrificial death and resurrection.

WEDNESDAY

John 10:14–18 The Shepherd Protects His Sheep

1. Who was Jesus obeying when he lay down his life (v. 18)?

   His Father.

2. What does verse 18 tell us about Christ's death?

   It tells us that he gave his life freely on the cross and that he took it back again in the resurrection.

God the Father willingly gave Christ, and Christ willingly gave his life to save his sheep.

Praise God the Father and God the Son for their joint commitment to save their sheep.

THURSDAY

John 13:1–7 The Servant Washes Feet

1. How long did Jesus's love last (v. 1)?

   To the very end.

2. What did Jesus do the last night before his death (v. 5)?

   He washed the disciples' feet.

Jesus's love did not waver. He demonstrated it on the eve of his death by washing the disciples' feet, giving us an example of service that we are to follow (vv. 14–15).

Thank Jesus for his love and for his servant spirit even at his lowest point, and pray that we would be able to show the same servant love to others.

FRIDAY

John 14:1–6 The Builder Prepares a Home

1. What is Jesus doing in heaven (v. 2)?

   He is preparing a place for his people.

2. How many ways are there to God (v. 6)?

   There is only one way to God: Jesus.

Jesus is the only way to God, the only source of truth, and the only fountain of life.

Pray for faith in Christ alone as the only way to God.

SATURDAY

John 15:1–8 The Vine Produces Grapes

1. What must we do to produce good fruit in our lives (v. 4)?

   Abide in Christ.

2. How much can we do without Christ (v. 5)?

   Nothing.

The only way to bear good fruit in our lives is by being united to Christ by faith.

Pray for fruitful lives through union with Christ by faith.

SUNDAY

Read the most important verses that your pastor preached on today.

What did you learn about God?

What did you learn about sin?

What did you learn about Jesus?

What did you learn about living?

What is the biggest lesson from the sermon?

What does the sermon lead us to pray for?

EXPEDITION 37
THE DARKEST NIGHT

OUR MAP

We're about to embark on the darkest part of our journey. We're going to walk alongside Jesus as he walks a path of suffering and death. After many years of teaching and healing, Jesus will be condemned to death. The light of the world will be put out by the darkness of the world. But don't fear: there is a happy ending to this saddest of stories.

 PRAYER POINTS

 SNAPSHOT VERSE
Matthew 26:28

MONDAY

Matthew 26:26–30 Jesus Covenants

1. What do the bread and wine picture (vv. 26–28)?

   Christ's body and blood.

2. What does Christ's blood secure (v. 28)?

   Remission (forgiveness) of sins.

Christ left us pictures of his death in the Lord's Supper to reassure us of his power to cancel our sins.

Pray that we would personally know the power of Christ to cancel sin in our lives.

TUESDAY

Matthew 26:31–35 Jesus Warns

1. What did Jesus say the disciples would do (v. 31)?

   He said they would fall away (or stumble).

2. What was behind Peter's insistence that he would never fall away (v. 33)?

   Overconfidence.

None of us are so strong that we could never stumble and fall like the disciples did.

Confess our weakness and our need for divine strengthening to stop us from falling.

WEDNESDAY

Matthew 26:36–41 Jesus Prays

1. What is the way to avoid temptation (v. 41)?

   Watch and pray.

2. Why did the disciples keep falling asleep (v. 41)?

   Although they had willing spirits, they were weak in their flesh.

Watching and praying is the way to strengthen our spiritual life.

Pray for watchfulness that will strengthen us to be vigilant rather than spiritually sleepy.

THURSDAY

Matthew 26:42–46 Jesus Prepares

1. What did Jesus pray (v. 42)?

   He prayed for this [the cup] to pass from him.

2. What should we do in the worst days of our lives?

   Pray to our heavenly Father.

The best preparation for our worst days is to pray to our heavenly Father.

Thank God that we can draw near to our heavenly Father even in the darkest times.

FRIDAY

Matthew 26:47–50 Jesus Is Betrayed

1. What did Judas do and say to Jesus (v. 49)?

   He greeted him and kissed him.

2. Why did Jesus call Judas "Friend" (v. 50)?

   It was his last attempt to reach his heart and turn him from sin to himself.

Jesus is the most loving person that ever existed, as evidenced by calling his betrayer "friend."

Thank Jesus for his offers of friendship even to his worst enemies.

SATURDAY

Matthew 26:51–56 Jesus Is Abandoned

1. What did the disciples do (v. 56)?

   They all forsook Jesus and ran away.

2. What tempts you to run away from Jesus?

   Talk about the kinds of pressures and stressors at school and among friends that make us want to run away from Jesus.

Although Jesus came to save sinners, even those he came to save ran away from him.

Pray for courage to trust Jesus even if others are running away from him.

SUNDAY

Read the most important verses that your pastor preached on today.

What did you learn about God?

What did you learn about sin?

What did you learn about Jesus?

What did you learn about living?

What is the biggest lesson from the sermon?

What does the sermon lead us to pray for?

EXPEDITION 38
THE DARKEST TRIAL

OUR MAP

Jesus was tried in a Jewish court, a royal court, and a Roman court. All three courts were unfair and unjust in condemning Jesus without any good reason.

 PRAYER POINTS

 SNAPSHOT VERSE
1 Peter 2:23

MONDAY

Matthew 26:57–61 Jesus Accused

 1. Describe the witnesses against Jesus (vv. 59–60).

   They were false witnesses who told lies about Jesus.

2. What was the aim of the Jewish leaders (v. 59)?

   They wanted to put him to death.

 Even the most truthful person in the world was the victim of lies.

 Pray that God would make us truth-tellers and that we would never be lie-tellers.

TUESDAY

Matthew 26:62-68 **Jesus Sentenced**

1. What was Jesus's response to the false accusations (v. 63)?

   He kept silent.

2. What was Jesus's last message to his accusers (v. 64)?

   He warned them of his coming again to judge the world.

Even though Jesus knew his accusers were trying to kill him, he did not defend himself, but rather warned them that divine judgment was coming to them.

Pray for self-control and trust in God no matter how much we are provoked and how many lies are told about us

WEDNESDAY

Matthew 26:69-75 **Jesus Denied**

1. What did Peter do when he denied Jesus (v. 74)?

   He cursed and swore.

2. What did Peter do when he realized his sin (v. 75)?

   He went out and wept bitterly.

When we sin, we should repent with sorrow.

Ask for courage to own Christ and grace never to deny him, and for courage to confess with sorrow if we do.

THURSDAY

Matthew 27:1–5 Jesus Delivered

1. What did Judas eventually realize (v. 4)?

   He realized he had betrayed innocent blood.

2. What did Judas do (v. 5)?

   He killed himself.

Even Jesus's worst enemies know in their hearts that he is a good person and feel guilty about their response to him.

Pray for true repentance that leads to Christ and life rather than just regret that leads away from Christ and to death.

FRIDAY

Matthew 27:12–18 Jesus Is Silent

1. Why was the governor amazed (v. 14)?

   Because Jesus did not answer the accusations.

2. What prophecy did this fulfill, particularly verses 12 and 14?

   Jesus remained silent (Isaiah 53:7).

Jesus's death fulfilled detailed Old Testament prophecies.

Thank God for the detailed prophecies that Christ's death fulfilled.

SATURDAY

Matthew 27:19–26 Jesus Exchanged

1. Whom did the people ask to be released instead of Jesus (vv. 20, 26)?

   An evil criminal called Barabbas.

2. What does the people's preference for Barabbas to be released tell us about humanity (John 3:19)?

   People love darkness rather than light because their actions are evil.

We love darkness rather than light because our actions are evil.

Confess our love for darkness more than light, our preference for lies more than truth, our preference for sin more than holiness.

SUNDAY

Read the most important verses that your pastor preached on today.

What did you learn about God?

_____

What did you learn about sin?

_____

What did you learn about Jesus?

_____

What did you learn about living?

_____

What is the biggest lesson from the sermon?

_____

What does the sermon lead us to pray for?

_____

EXPEDITION 39
THE DARKEST DEATH

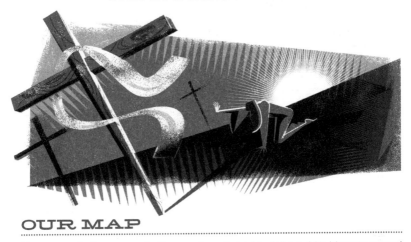

OUR MAP

The scene darkens even further as Jesus's trial is followed by his torture and murder on a cross.

 PRAYER POINTS

 SNAPSHOT VERSE
Luke 23:42

MONDAY

Matthew 27:27–33 Jesus Stripped

 1. What did the soldiers put on Jesus's head (v. 29)?

A crown of thorns.

2. How did Jesus respond to the mockery? (1 Peter 2:23)?

He did not retaliate but committed himself to God as his perfect judge.

 Jesus is the perfect model of restraint in the face of the worst provocation.

 Praise Jesus for his willingness to endure this suffering so perfectly and provide such a perfect model for us when we face our own mockers and persecutors.

TUESDAY

Matthew 27:34–38 Jesus Crucified

1. What did the soldiers write above the cross (v. 37)?

   This is Jesus, the King of the Jews.

2. What is true about this statement?

   It is half true. He is King of the Jews, but he is also King of the Gentiles.

Christ's kingly glory is founded upon his suffering humiliation.

Ask for grace to bow to Jesus as our King because of what he suffered for sinners like us.

WEDNESDAY

Matthew 27:39–44 Jesus Mocked

1. What did the robbers do (v. 44)?

   They reviled (insulted) Jesus.

2. What prophecy did verse 44 fulfill (Isaiah 53:12)?

   Jesus was numbered with the transgressors.

Jesus is willing to be counted amongst the worst criminals in order to save the worst criminals.

Praise Jesus for his willingness to be counted not just among the human race but among the worst of humans in order to save them.

THURSDAY

Luke 23:39–43 Jesus Saves

1. What did one of the dying thieves say to Jesus (v. 42)?

   He asked Jesus to remember him in his kingdom.

2. What did Jesus say to the repentant thief (v. 43)?

   He told him that he would be with him today in paradise.

It's never too late to turn from our sins and cast ourselves upon the mercy of Christ.

Plead with the Lord to save the worst people, even at the last moment.

FRIDAY

Matthew 27:45–49 Jesus Forsaken

1. What did Jesus say to God (v. 46)?

   He asked why God had forsaken him.

2. Why did Jesus have to suffer this forsakenness?

   Because we deserve to be abandoned by God for our sins.

Jesus was willing to experience even God's abandonment in order that we might enjoy God's nearness.

Confess that we deserve abandonment and ask for faith to believe that Christ suffered that for sinners.

SATURDAY

Matthew 27:50–56 Jesus Dies

1. What were some of the amazing signs that accompanied Jesus's death (vv. 51–52)?

   <u>The curtain of the temple was torn in two, there was a great earthquake, and some of the dead saints rose to life.</u>

2. What did the centurion say when he saw all these signs (v. 54)?

   <u>He said that this was truly the Son of God.</u>

Christ's death shook the whole world but it also shook the inner world of the centurion.

Pray that the death of Christ would continue to impact people today, turning them to faith in God.

SUNDAY

Read the most important verses that your pastor preached on today.

What did you learn about God?

_____

What did you learn about sin?

_____

What did you learn about Jesus?

_____

What did you learn about living?

_____

What is the biggest lesson from the sermon?

_____

What does the sermon lead us to pray for?

_____

EXPEDITION 40
THE BRIGHTEST MORNING

OUR MAP

The King is dead. Long live the King! Although the past expedition was shrouded in darkness as Jesus was crucified, in this expedition we'll see the sun rise again and shine more brightly than ever.

 PRAYER POINTS

 SNAPSHOT VERSE
Matthew 28:19

MONDAY

Matthew 27:57-61 A Dead Body

1. What did Joseph do with Jesus's body (v. 60)?

   <u>He laid it in his tomb.</u>

2. How did Joseph close the tomb (v. 60)?

   <u>By rolling a large stone against the door.</u>

Jesus has gone before us in his suffering, in his death, and in his burial.

Thank God that Jesus tasted death to save us from death (Hebrews 2:9).

TUESDAY

Matthew 27:62–66 A Sealed Tomb

1. What did the Pharisees remember (v. 63)?

   They remembered that Jesus had said he would rise after three days.

2. What did the Pharisees do to the tomb (v. 66)?

   They sealed it securely and set a guard.

God used the Pharisees to prove that Jesus was dead and that no one stole the body.

Praise God that he overrules evil plans to fulfill his good plan.

WEDNESDAY

Matthew 28:1–4 An Open Tomb

1. Who rolled away the stone (v. 2)?

   An angel of the Lord.

2. What was the impact on the guards (v. 4)?

   They shook and became like dead men.

The resurrection of Christ is terrifying to the ungodly.

Ask God that many of the ungodly will put their trust in the risen Lord so that the resurrection will be a comfort to them and not a terror.

THURSDAY

Matthew 28:5–8 An Empty Tomb

1. What are the most wonderful words in the universe (v. 6)?

   He is not here, for he has risen.

2. What does the women's reaction teach us (v. 8)?

   That we should respond to Christ's resurrection with joy and excitement.

The resurrection of Christ is a source of excitement and joy to the godly.

Pray that God would give us great joy and awe as we think about the resurrection of Christ and of ourselves.

FRIDAY

Matthew 28:9–15 A Great Celebration

1. What did the women do when they saw Jesus (v. 9)?

   They held him by the feet and worshiped him.

2. What did Jesus say to the women (v. 10)?

   He told them not to be afraid but to tell his disciples to meet him in Galilee.

The resurrection of Christ produces worship and reduces fear.

Pray to know more and more of the power of Christ's resurrection in our lives, producing worship and reducing fear (Philippians 3:10).

SATURDAY

Matthew 28:16–20 A Great Commission

1. What command did Jesus give the disciples (v. 19)?

   <u>He told them to go into all the world, making disciples, baptizing, and teaching.</u>

2. What is the great comfort that Christ gives to those obey his great commission (v. 20)?

   <u>He promises to be with us.</u>

When Jesus gives a difficult command, he gives a comforting promise to the obedient.

Pray for obedience to Christ's command and faith in Christ's promise.

SUNDAY

Read the most important verses that your pastor preached on today.

What did you learn about God?

What did you learn about sin?

What did you learn about Jesus?

What did you learn about living?

What is the biggest lesson from the sermon?

What does the sermon lead us to pray for?

EXPEDITION 41
THE GOSPEL FOR THE WORLD

OUR MAP

Up until now, our expeditions have been mainly centered on Israel, a small country in the Middle East. Now, the apostles are about to take the gospel into all the world as Jesus commanded them. The book of Acts begins with Jesus ascending to heaven and giving his disciples two promises. The first is that they would receive the Holy Spirit to make them witnesses to Christ (Acts 1:8). The second was that he would return again to earth in the same way he had left it (Acts 1:11). This brings us to the day of Pentecost, when the first of these promises would be fulfilled in a wonderful way.

 PRAYER POINTS

 SNAPSHOT VERSE
Acts 2:21

MONDAY

Acts 2:1–6 Full of the Spirit

1. What were the disciples filled with (v. 4)?

   <u>The Holy Spirit.</u>

2. What do the special signs of Pentecost teach us (vv. 2–3)?

   <u>They teach us that the pouring out of the Holy Spirit was a very special event.</u>

One of God's greatest gifts to his people is the pouring out of the Holy Spirit

Pray for the Holy Spirit to be poured out in power again and again.

TUESDAY

Acts 2:7-13 Full of Wine?

1. What amazed the people (vv. 7-8)?

   <u>People were amazed that they could understand the apostles in their own languages.</u>

2. What was the apostles' message (v. 11)?

   <u>The wonderful works of God.</u>

When the Holy Spirit is present, people will be taken up with the wonderful works of God.

Ask to be amazed at the wonderful works of God rather than mock them (vv. 12-13).

WEDNESDAY

Acts 2:14-21 Full of Courage

1. Which prophet's prediction came true at Pentecost (v. 16)?

   <u>The prophet Joel (see Joel 2:27-32).</u>

2. What is God's promise to those who call on the name of the Lord (v. 21)?

   <u>They will be saved.</u>

The gospel promises us that if we call upon the name of the Lord, we will be saved.

Pray for many to call upon the Lord and embrace his promise of salvation.

THURSDAY

Acts 2:22–24, 36–39 Full of Good News

1. What was the result of Peter charging the people with murdering Jesus (v. 37)?

   They were convicted in their hearts and cried out, "What shall we do?"

2. What was Peter's message to them (v. 38)?

   Repent and be baptized in the name of Jesus to receive the forgiveness of sins and the gift of the Holy Spirit.

When we are convicted of sin, if we repent, we will be fully forgiven and empowered with the Holy Spirit.

Ask for the Holy Spirit both to convict of sin and to fill with spiritual power.

FRIDAY

Acts 2:40–43 Full of Believers

1. How many people were converted to Christ that day (v. 41)?

   Three thousand.

2. What happens when people are converted to Christ (v. 42)?

   They continue steadfastly in the apostles' teaching and fellowship, in the breaking of bread, and in prayers.

When people are converted to Christ, they join the church of Christ.

Ask God to bless the church with conversions and with loyalty to the church.

SATURDAY

Acts 2:44–47 Full of Love

1. What did people do with their possessions (vv. 44–45)?

   They sold everything and shared the proceeds with the other believers.

2. Describe the early church (vv. 46–47).

   They were united and happy in eating together, living together, and praising God.

True Christianity results in loving unity and united love.

Pray for Christian love in the church that will unite people in every way.

SUNDAY

Read the most important verses that your pastor preached on today.

What did you learn about God?

_____

What did you learn about sin?

_____

What did you learn about Jesus?

_____

What did you learn about living?

_____

What is the biggest lesson from the sermon?

_____

What does the sermon lead us to pray for?

_____

EXPEDITION 42
THE MOST FAMOUS ROAD
IN THE WORLD

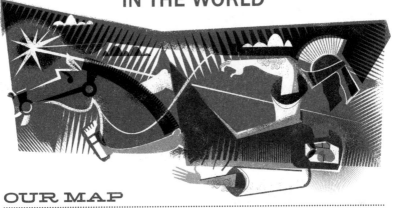

OUR MAP

Have you ever heard of the Damascus Road? The most famous conversion happened there. Let's travel along it and see what God did to change Saul of Tarsus into the apostle Paul.

 PRAYER POINTS

 SNAPSHOT VERSE
Acts 9:15

MONDAY

Acts 9:1–5 Persecuting Saul

 1. What was Saul's first question (v. 5)?

He asked who was speaking to him.

2. How is persecuting Christians the same as persecuting Christ (v. 5)?

Because Christ regards Christians as part of his body.

 Jesus loves his people so much that he views them as part of his body (1 Corinthians 6:15).

 Pray that persecuted Christians would be comforted by knowing they are Christ's body.

TUESDAY

Acts 9:6–9 Blind Saul

1. What instructions did Jesus give to Saul (v. 6)?

   <u>**To enter the city and wait for more instructions.**</u>

2. How did Saul react to what he saw and heard (v. 9)?

   <u>**He was blinded for three days and did not eat or drink.**</u>

It is an evidence of faith in Christ when we stop asking what *we* want to do and start asking what *Christ* wants us to do.

Ask the Lord what he wants you to do today and with your whole life.

WEDNESDAY

Acts 9:10–16 Chosen Saul

1. Why was Ananias scared of Saul (vv. 13–14)?

   <u>**Because Saul had previously persecuted Christians.**</u>

2. What was God's purpose for Saul (v. 15)?

   <u>**He chose him to carry his name to many people.**</u>

God has chosen us to be carriers of his name to others.

Ask God for help to carry Christ's name to others.

THURSDAY

Acts 9:17–20 Preaching Saul

1. What was Ananias's first word to Saul (v. 17)?

   He called him "brother."

2. What did Saul do as soon as he got his sight and strength back (v. 20)?

   He preached Christ, that he is the Son of God.

Only the Lord Jesus can make the greatest enemy of Christians into a brother of Christians and a preacher of Christ.

Thank God for his converting power and pray for more enemies of Christ to be transformed into brothers in Christ and preachers of Christ.

FRIDAY

Acts 9:21–25 Growing Saul

1. What did Saul prove (v. 22)?

   He proved that Jesus is the Christ.

2. How can we prove that Jesus is the Christ?

   By doing what Paul did, showing that the Old Testament prophecies of the Messiah (the Christ) were fulfilled in Jesus.

Jesus perfectly fulfills the Old Testament prophecies.

Praise God for how Jesus perfectly matches the Old Testament prophecies and pray for those trying to persuade others that Jesus is the Christ.

SATURDAY

Acts 9:26–31 Courageous Saul

1. Who persuaded the disciples that Saul had been converted (v. 27)?

   Barnabas.

2. Describe the church in verse 31.

   They were edified, walked in the fear of the Lord, were comforted by the Holy Spirit, and multiplied.

Our churches should match the description in verse 31.

Pray for our churches to match the New Testament models more closely.

SUNDAY

Read the most important verses that your pastor preached on today.

What did you learn about God?

What did you learn about sin?

What did you learn about Jesus?

What did you learn about living?

What is the biggest lesson from the sermon?

What does the sermon lead us to pray for?

EXPEDITION 43
THREE CONVERSIONS

OUR MAP

After his conversion, the apostle Paul traveled everywhere preaching Christ. As a result, Saul the persecutor became Paul the persecuted. In Acts 16, he ends up in the Philippi jail. But he also sees three people converted to Christ: a businesswoman, a slave girl, and a jailer. Three very different people. Three very different conversions.

 PRAYER POINTS

 SNAPSHOT VERSE
Acts 16:31

MONDAY

Acts 16:9–15 Salvation by the River

 1. How was Lydia saved (v. 14)?

The Lord opened her heart.

2. What does this tell us about our hearts?

It tells us that before conversion our hearts are closed to the Lord, but he powerfully and graciously opens them.

 The Lord can open our hearts to receive his word and his servants.

 Confess that our hearts are closed and hardened against God, thank God if our hearts have been opened, and ask God to open many more closed hearts.

TUESDAY

Acts 16:16–19 Salvation on the Street

1. What did the slave girl cry out (v. 17)?

   These men are the servants of the Most High God who proclaim the way of salvation.

2. How was the girl saved (v. 18)?

   Paul commanded the evil spirit to come out in the name of the Lord Jesus.

The name of the Lord Jesus is the most powerful force for good in the world.

May all of our prayers end with "in Jesus's name."

WEDNESDAY

Acts 16:20–24 Sentenced to Jail

1. What were Paul and Silas falsely accused of (v. 21)?

   Teaching customs against Roman law.

2. How were Paul and Silas punished (vv. 22–23)?

   They were stripped, beaten, and put in prison.

We can expect to be falsely accused and wrongly punished for being a faithful Christian witness.

Pray for those suffering for their faith, that God would sustain them and keep them faithful.

THURSDAY

Acts 16:25–28 Singing in Jail

1. What did Paul and Silas do in the jail (v. 25)?

   <u>They prayed and sang hymns.</u>

2. What command of Jesus were they obeying (Matthew 5:11–12)?

   <u>The command to rejoice and be glad even in the midst of persecution.</u>

God's people are blessed with joy even in the midst of sufferings for the sake of Christ.

Ask God to give his people glad songs in the midst of sufferings.

FRIDAY

Acts 16:29–34 Salvation in Jail

1. What must we do to be saved (v. 31)?

   <u>Believe in the Lord Jesus Christ.</u>

2. Why was the jailer so happy (v. 34)?

   <u>Because he had believed in God with all his household.</u>

Faith in Christ saves and rejoices the heart.

Ask the Lord to give us saving and joyful faith.

SATURDAY

Acts 16:35–40 Encouraged in Lydia's House

1. What did Paul and Silas do when they were released (v. 40)?

   They went to Lydia's house and encouraged the other Christians.

2. How can we encourage other Christians?

   Like Paul and Silas, we can share what God has done in our lives and other's lives.

There is nothing more encouraging than hearing about God's saving of sinners.

Pray for more conversions of people in prayer meetings, people in false religion, people in prisons, and people in many other places too.

SUNDAY

Read the most important verses that your pastor preached on today.

What did you learn about God?

_____

What did you learn about sin?

_____

What did you learn about Jesus?

_____

What did you learn about living?

_____

What is the biggest lesson from the sermon?

_____

What does the sermon lead us to pray for?

_____

EXPEDITION 44
ATHENS

OUR MAP

Having traveled hundreds of miles preaching the gospel and starting churches, Paul finds himself in Athens (Acts 17). As he walks around, he gets sad and angry about all the idols and all the people worshiping them. You won't be surprised to find out that soon he's preaching the gospel to them.

 PRAYER POINTS

 SNAPSHOT VERSE
Acts 17:30

MONDAY

Acts 17:1–4 Some Were Persuaded

1. What did Paul usually do when he came to a city (vv. 1–2)?

   <u>He went to the synagogue and reasoned from the Scriptures.</u>

2. Some were persuaded to follow Christ (vv. 4–5). What persuaded you to follow Christ, or why are you not persuaded to follow Christ?

   <u>Discuss these questions with your family.</u>

The best way to persuade someone to become a follower of Christ is to reason with them from the Scriptures.

Pray that God would bless preachers as they persuade people to follow Christ by reasoning from the Scriptures.

TUESDAY

Acts 17:5-8 Some Were Angry

1. Why did the Jews who were not persuaded attack the apostles (v. 5)?

   Because they were envious of them.

2. What did the Jews of Thessalonica accuse the apostles of doing (v. 6)?

   They said they had turned the world upside down.

Even though the Christian message is one of peace, we will be accused of disrupting society and we will be attacked.

Ask God for courage to be a Christian witness no matter what people say about us or do to us.

WEDNESDAY

Acts 17:10-15 Some Were Students

1. How did the Bereans respond to the apostles' message (v. 11)?

   They received the word and searched the Scriptures to see if the apostles were telling the truth.

2. How can you be like the Bereans?

   By receiving God's message through his servants but also by making sure they are telling the truth by comparing what they say with the Scriptures.

The Bereans are an example of how to hear preaching by receiving it and by checking it with the Scriptures.

Ask God to make us like the Bereans.

THURSDAY

Acts 17:16–21 Some Were Curious

1. How did Paul react to all the idols (v. 16)?

His spirit was provoked and stirred up.

2. What did the Athenians and the foreigners spend their time doing (v. 21)?

Telling and hearing new things.

We ought to listen to the reliable word of God rather than always be searching for new ideas about religion.

Ask God to make us satisfied with his word and resistant to novelty.

FRIDAY

Acts 17:22–28 Some Were Religious

1. What did the inscription on the altar say (v. 23)?

"To the unknown god."

2. How does Paul describe people's relationship to God (v. 28)?

"In him we live and move and have our being."

God has made himself known even to those without the Bible so that they might seek him (v. 27).

Pray that God would stir up people to seek him and to find that he is not far from anyone.

SATURDAY

Acts 17:29–34 Some Were Mockers

1. What does God command everyone (v. 30)?

   God commands everyone to repent.

2. What is God commanding you to repent of? Ask your family to identify specific sins to repent of.

God commands everyone to repent now because he is coming to judge the world by Jesus Christ (v. 31).

Pray for a spirit of repentance, that many would turn from sin to God before the final judgment.

SUNDAY

Read the most important verses that your pastor preached on today.

What did you learn about God?

_____

What did you learn about sin?

_____

What did you learn about Jesus?

_____

What did you learn about living?

_____

What is the biggest lesson from the sermon?

_____

What does the sermon lead us to pray for?

_____

EXPEDITION 45
PREACHING TO THE KING

After three eventful missionary journeys, the apostle Paul decided to go to Jerusalem and Rome to preach (Acts 19:21). Although his friends warned him against this, he said that he was even ready to die in Jerusalem for the name of the Lord Jesus (Acts 21:1–13). As expected, he was arrested there and sent to prison. After being tried in front of various judges (Acts 22–25), he was summoned to appear before King Agrippa in Caesarea (Acts 26). Let's listen in on Paul's thrilling defense before the king.

 PRAYER POINTS

 SNAPSHOT VERSE
Acts 26:18

MONDAY

Acts 26:1–8 I Was a Jew

1. Why was Paul being judged (v. 6)?

   For his hope in God's promise.

2. What is the promise he is hoping in (vv. 7–8)?

   The hope of the resurrection of the dead.

God's promise of resurrection from the dead is a long-standing promise dating back to Old Testament times.

Thank God for his promises, and pray for hope in his promise of resurrection from the dead through Jesus Christ.

TUESDAY

Acts 26:9–11 I Was a Persecutor

1. What was Paul doing before he became a Christian (v. 9)?

   He was opposing Jesus Christ.

2. Paul opposed Christ by persecuting his people (vv. 10–11). What other ways do people oppose Christ?

   Refusing to listen to him, trust him, believe in him, or follow him.

Before we are converted, we are opponents to Christ and express that opposition in various ways.

With Paul, let us confess our preconversion opposition to Christ, thank him if he has made us his followers now, and pray for those that are still opposing him.

WEDNESDAY

Acts 26:12–18 I Am a Christian

1. Why was Paul sent to the Gentiles (v. 18)?

   To open their eyes, to turn them from darkness to light, and to turn them from Satan's power to God's, so that they can be forgiven and go to heaven.

2. What has God opened your eyes to? What darkness has he turned you from? How can you see God's power defeating Satan's power in your life?

   Have a conversation with your family about these questions.

Conversion results in massive changes in our lives, in our standing before God, and in our destiny.

Thank God for the revolutionary power of conversion.

191

THURSDAY

Acts 26:19–23 I Am a Preacher

 1. Where did Paul get his help to preach (v. 22)?

From God.

2. What was the message from Paul, the prophets, and Moses (v. 23)?

That Christ would suffer, rise from the dead, and preach light to all.

 The New Testament gospel message is the same as the Old Testament gospel message.

 Ask God to give us a clear understanding of the gospel as taught by both the Old and New Testaments.

FRIDAY

Acts 26:24–29 I Am Not Crazy

 1. How did King Agrippa respond to Paul's preaching (v. 28)?

He was almost persuaded to become a Christian.

2. Are you unpersuaded, almost persuaded, or fully persuaded about Christ?

 Even the best preacher in the world relies on God to persuade people to become Christians.

 Ask God to add his persuasive power to the preaching of the gospel so that people are fully persuaded.

SATURDAY

Acts 26:30–32; 28:16, 30–31 I Am a Prisoner

1. What did Paul do in Rome when he was kept as a prisoner in a house (Acts 28:31)?

   <u>He preached the kingdom of God and taught about Jesus Christ.</u>

2. How did he do this (v. 31)?

   <u>With all boldness, and he would not let anyone stop him.</u>

No amount of suffering, persecution, or imprisonment could stop Paul from boldly preaching Christ.

Pray for Paul's courageous spirit so that we keep witnessing for Christ no matter where we are.

SUNDAY

Read the most important verses that your pastor preached on today.

What did you learn about God?

What did you learn about sin?

What did you learn about Jesus?

What did you learn about living?

What is the biggest lesson from the sermon?

What does the sermon lead us to pray for?

EXPEDITION 46
OLD FAITHFUL

OUR MAP

The apostle Paul sent a letter to the Roman Christians years before he arrived in Rome as a prisoner. In his letter he wrote about how much he longed to see and fellowship with them. Little did he think that he would arrive in chains! This letter contains many beautiful sections, but we have time to look at only one part. It's like having only one day to explore Yellowstone National Park. It's a difficult choice, but I've decided to lead you through Romans 8. This chapter in Romans is like the Old Faithful geyser at Yellowstone. It's deep, high, and full of power, and you never tire of looking at it.

 PRAYER POINTS

 SNAPSHOT VERSE
Romans 8:28

MONDAY

Romans 8:1–5 Walking in the Spirit

 1. What kind of people are not condemned by God (v. 1)?

Those who are in Christ Jesus.

2. What are the two main subjects in people's thoughts (v. 5)?

Worldly (fleshly) things or spiritual things.

 Peace with God through Jesus Christ is the foundation for a peaceful and spiritual mind.

 Ask God to take away our condemnation by uniting us with Christ and to give us his Spirit so that we have a spiritual mind.

TUESDAY

Romans 8:11–17 Led by the Spirit

1. What does the Holy Spirit help us to say to God (v. 15)?

   Abba, Father.

2. What does the Holy Spirit say in our hearts (v. 16)?

   That we are children of God.

The Holy Spirit helps Christians to call God "Father" and assures them that they are his children.

Ask for the Holy Spirit so that we will be able to call God "Father" and have much assurance of being his children.

WEDNESDAY

Romans 8:18–25 Groaning by the Spirit

1. What does Paul compare present sufferings with (v. 18)?

   He says that the present sufferings do not compare with future glory.

2. What do Christians groan for (v. 23)?

   The redemption of our body.

Whatever present sufferings our bodies experience, God will redeem our bodies in glory.

Ask God for help to hope for future bodily redemption especially when we groan over present bodily sufferings.

THURSDAY

Romans 8:26-30 Helped by the Spirit

1. How does the Holy Spirit help us (v. 26)?

   He helps us in our weaknesses.

2. Give an example of all things working together for the good of God's people (v. 28).

   Think of a bad situation that turned out good in the end or a bad event that had some good results.

God strengthens his weak people with the help of the Holy Spirit and with the help of his promise that all things work together for good.

Ask God to strengthen us with his Holy Spirit and his promises.

FRIDAY

Romans 8:31-34 No Accusation

1. Complete this sentence: If God is for us, _____ (v. 31).

2. Where is Christ and what is he doing (v. 34)?

   He is at God's right hand praying for his people.

God is for us and therefore nothing can be against us. Christ prays for us and therefore nothing can condemn us.

Praise God that he is for us and that he will not let any accusation stand against us because Christ prays for his people.

SATURDAY

Romans 8:35–39 No Separation

1. What can separate us from the love of Christ (vv. 38–39)?

   Nothing.

2. What do you fear could separate you from the love of Christ, and how does the promise of Romans 8:38–39 help you overcome that fear?

   Identify your greatest fear and show from the list in verses 38–39 that Christ's love is more powerful than the greatest danger.

Although many things try to separate us from Christ's love, nothing can.

Thank God for the unbreakable and inseparable love of Christ and pray for a deep sense of security from it.

SUNDAY

Read the most important verses that your pastor preached on today.

What did you learn about God?

_____

What did you learn about sin?

_____

What did you learn about Jesus?

_____

What did you learn about living?

_____

What is the biggest lesson from the sermon?

_____

What does the sermon lead us to pray for?

_____

EXPEDITION 47
THE WAY OF LOVE

OUR MAP

The church in Corinth was divided. People were fighting with one another and following different preachers instead of following God. In his first letter to the Corinthians, the apostle Paul reminded the Christians there to focus on Christ not preachers (chap. 1), and to love one another as Christ loved the church (chap. 13). He also defended the Bible's teaching about the resurrection, which some in Corinth were denying (chap. 15).

 PRAYER POINTS

 SNAPSHOT VERSE
1 Corinthians 15:21

MONDAY

1 Corinthians 1:18–25 God's Wisdom

 1. How do people react to the message of the cross (v. 18)?

Some say it is foolishness, and others say it is the power of God.

2. What is the message of the cross to you?

Weakness, foolishness, or power?

 Although some see the cross as evidence of weakness and foolishness, believers see it as evidence of God's wisdom and power.

 Pray that the cross of Christ would be a powerful influence in our lives.

TUESDAY

1 Corinthians 1:26–31 God's Choice

1. Who did God choose to save in Corinth (v. 27)?

   The weak and the foolish.

2. What should we glory in or boast about (v. 31)?

   We should boast or glory in the Lord alone.

If it is God's choice that ultimately saves us, then we should not boast in ourselves but only in God.

Pray that God would help us boast not in ourselves but in him alone.

WEDNESDAY

1 Corinthians 13:1–7 God's Love

1. What does love not do (vv. 4–6)?

   It is not _____

2. What ways can you show this kind of love?

   Give some practical examples, even within the family.

Although Christ alone can live up to this definition of love, he calls us to follow his example.

Confess our failures to love in this way, thank Christ for his perfect love, and ask for grace to love like he loved.

THURSDAY

1 Corinthians 13:8–13 God's Face

1. Which is the greatest: faith, hope, or love (v. 13)?

   Love.

2. One day we will see Christ and his love face-to-face (v. 12). What are you most looking forward to seeing?

   Talk about this expectation and experience.

One day our dim and distant experience of Christ's love will be replaced with face-to-face communion with his love.

Praise God that death will be the beginning of a new and far deeper experience of Christ's love and that it will last forever.

FRIDAY

1 Corinthians 15:12–19 God's Resurrection

1. What is Christian hope built upon (v. 14)?

   Christian hope is built upon the resurrection of Christ.

2. What would be the result if Christ is not risen from the dead (v. 17)?

   Our faith is pointless, and we are still in our sins.

The resurrection of Christ is critical to Christian faith and hope.

Pray for strong faith in Christ's resurrection and the defeat of all false teachers who deny this vital truth.

SATURDAY

1 Corinthians 15:20–26 God's Victory

1. Where will Christ put his enemies (v. 25)?

   Under his feet.

2. What is the last enemy that God will destroy (v. 26)?

   Death.

Christ will defeat all his enemies, including our great enemy, death.

Pray for the day when Christ will defeat every enemy, especially death, and will reign over all as the everlasting King.

SUNDAY

Read the most important verses that your pastor preached on today.

What did you learn about God?

What did you learn about sin?

What did you learn about Jesus?

What did you learn about living?

What is the biggest lesson from the sermon?

What does the sermon lead us to pray for?

EXPEDITION 48
THREE APPETIZERS

OUR MAP

Paul wrote short letters to the churches in Galatia, Ephesus, and Philippi, each one packed full of precious truth. We don't have time to read them all in an expedition that lasts just a week, but I hope that the brief samples we'll taste will give you an appetite for more.

 PRAYER POINTS

 SNAPSHOT VERSE
Philippians 2:10-11

MONDAY

Galatians 5:14-21 Rotten Fruit

 1. How is the Christian to walk (v. 16)?

By the Spirit.

2. What will happen to those whose lives are full of the works of the flesh (vv. 19-21)?

They will not inherit the kingdom of God.

 Without the Holy Spirit, our lives will bear rotten fruit and we will end outside the kingdom of God.

 Ask for the Holy Spirit to drive the works of the flesh out of our lives and to purge our lives of rotten fruit.

TUESDAY

Galatians 5:22–26 Good Fruit

1. List the good fruit that the Holy Spirit produces (vv. 22–23).

   Love, joy, peace, patience, kindness, goodness, faithfulness, gentleness, and self-control.

2. Which of these good spiritual fruits are in your life?

   Talk about what fruits are there, what ones are absent, and how to change this.

The Holy Spirit is our only hope of a fruit-bearing life.

Ask for the Holy Spirit to grow good spiritual fruit in our lives.

WEDNESDAY

Ephesians 5:22–27 Husbands and Wives

1. What did Christ do for the church (v. 25)?

   He loved her and gave himself up for her.

2. What is a husband to do for his wife (v. 25)?

   He is to love his wife and give himself up for her.

Christ's person and work is to be our model for a happy and holy marriage.

Pray for God's blessing on marriages, especially that they be modeled on Christ's relationship to his church.

THURSDAY

Ephesians 5:28–33 Christ and the Church

1. How are husbands to love their wives (v. 28)?

   As their own bodies.

2. What can we learn about Christ from marriage? What can we learn about marriage from Christ?

   Discuss this picture of marriage with your family.

God uses the illustration of married love to show how he loves and draws people to himself.

Pray that God would draw people into marriage with Christ.

FRIDAY

Philippians 2:1–4 Our Problem of Selfishness

1. How should you view others (v. 3)?

   As better than ourselves.

2. How can we look out for the interests of others (v. 4)?

   Give examples of how brothers and sisters can do this in the family.

We are called to esteem others better than ourselves and to look out for the interests of others as well as our own.

Ask God for an unselfish spirit in our thoughts and our actions.

SATURDAY

Philippians 2:5–11 Christ's Solution of Humility

 1. Whose mind is to be in us (v. 5)?

Christ's mind.

2. We can see Christ's mind in his selfless serving of others (vv. 6–8). How can you show Christ's selfless mind in your life?

Give examples in the home and the school.

 Christ's mind was always thinking about selfless service of others, and he calls us to a similar mind-set.

 Pray for Christ's mind-set of selfless service.

SUNDAY

Read the most important verses that your pastor preached on today.

 What did you learn about God?

_____

What did you learn about sin?

_____

What did you learn about Jesus?

_____

What did you learn about living?

_____

What is the biggest lesson from the sermon?

_____

What does the sermon lead us to pray for?

_____

EXPEDITION 49
THE HALL OF FAITH

OUR MAP

Many expeditions ago, we met a number of Old Testament heroes. Well, they're back! The letter to the Hebrews shows us that the Old Testament heroes were also believers. They had faith in God's promised Savior just like we do. They looked forward to him; we look back to him. But we are all looking to Jesus. The letter to the Hebrews also shows us how the Old Testament prophecies were ful-filled perfectly in the New Testament story of Jesus. Jesus is God's final sacrifice, God's final priest, God's final tabernacle, and God's final covenant.

 PRAYER POINTS

 SNAPSHOT VERSE
Hebrews 11:6

_____

_____

MONDAY

Hebrews 11:1–6 Faith Pleases God

 1. What does faith help us to understand (v. 3)?

It helps us to understand how God made the world from nothing.

2. If we do not have faith, what is impossible (v. 6)?

It is impossible to please God.

 No matter what we might do, if we do not have faith in Christ, we cannot please God.

 Ask for the kind of faith that pleases God.

TUESDAY

Hebrews 11:7-12 Faith Looks for a City

1. How did Abraham obey God's call to leave his home (v. 8)?

   By faith.

2. What was Abraham looking forward to (v. 10)?

   A city built by God, which is heaven.

Saving faith obeys God and looks beyond this world, to heaven.

Ask God for the kind of faith that obeys him and hopes for heaven.

WEDNESDAY

Hebrews 11:13-16 Faith Helps Us to Die

1. How did the Old Testament heroes die (v. 13)?

   In faith.

2. Believers confess that we are pilgrims on earth (v. 13). What does it mean to be a pilgrim?

   A pilgrim is only passing through this world to a better world and therefore does not get too attached to this world.

The faith of God's people not only helps them to die well but also to live well as pilgrims on this earth.

Confess that we get too attached to this world and ask God for help to live as faithful pilgrims.

THURSDAY

Hebrews 11:17–22 Faith Believes in Life after Death

1. What was Abraham thinking when he was about to sacrifice his son, Isaac (v. 19)?

   <u>That God was able to raise him from the dead.</u>

2. What do you look forward to about the resurrection?

   <u>Talk about how our bodies are weak, diseased, disabled, and decaying and how the resurrection will change that.</u>

God's people have always believed in the resurrection of the body, and this belief has had a powerful impact on this present life and our future hope.

Pray that God will keep us focused on the ultimate completion of salvation, the resurrection of our bodies in perfection.

FRIDAY

Hebrews 11:23–28 Faith Chooses Christ

1. What did Moses choose (v. 26)?

   <u>He chose the reproach of Christ instead of the treasures of Egypt.</u>

2. What characterized Moses (vv. 24, 27–29)?

   <u>Faith.</u>

Moses was an exemplary believer whose faith in the coming Christ not only saved him but enabled him to be a great teacher and leader of God's people.

Ask for help to choose Christ even when offered many temptations to choose the world.

SATURDAY

Hebrews 11:32–40 Faith Conquers Kingdoms

1. Who else were believers in the Old Testament (v. 32)?

   <u>Gideon, Barak, Samson, Jephthah, David, Samuel, and the prophets.</u>

2. What did they obtain (v. 39)?

   <u>They all obtained a good report and were commended through their faith.</u>

Let us aim for a good report by faith in God's word and in God's Savior.

Pray for the kind of faith that God will give a good report of.

SUNDAY

Read the most important verses that your pastor preached on today.

What did you learn about God?

_____

What did you learn about sin?

_____

What did you learn about Jesus?

_____

What did you learn about living?

_____

What is the biggest lesson from the sermon?

_____

What does the sermon lead us to pray for?

_____

EXPEDITION 50
A BURNING TONGUE AND
A BURNING WORLD

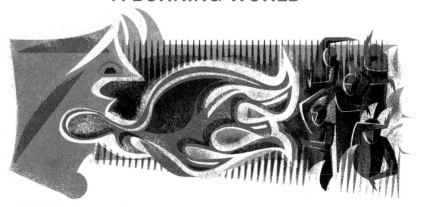

OUR MAP

Paul was not the only letter-writer. James, Peter, and John also wrote letters. They didn't write as many as Paul, and their letters were not as long as Paul's were. Let's look at some of the best-known chapters in their letters.

 PRAYER POINTS

 SNAPSHOT VERSE
1 John 1:7

MONDAY

James 3:1–5 The Tongue Boasts

 1. Describe the tongue (v. 5).

A little member that boasts great things.

2. In what ways have you misused your tongue, especially in boasting?

Give some examples.

 Although the tongue is small, it is very powerful and influential.

 Confess the sins of our tongues, especially our sins of boasting.

TUESDAY

James 3:6–12 **The Tongue Burns**

1. Who can tame the tongue (v. 8)?

   No ordinary person.

2. What should our tongues not do (v. 10)?

   We ought not to use our tongues for both cursing people and blessing God because these are opposites.

We need God to help us use our tongues in ways that please him.

Pray that God would keep us from cursing people and help us bless him with our tongues.

WEDNESDAY

2 Peter 3:1–7 **The World Was Flooded**

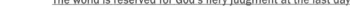

1. What does Peter warn us about (vv. 3–4)?

   He warns us about religious scoffers in the last days.

2. What is going to happen to this world at the last day (v. 7)?

   The world is reserved for God's fiery judgment at the last day.

The last days of this world will be very dangerous, and are closer than we think.

Ask God to protect us from enemies in the last days and to remind us daily that this world will be burned up.

THURSDAY

2 Peter 3:8–13 The World Will Burn

1. Why does Peter describe the Lord's coming back to judge as a thief in the night (v. 10)?

   Because it will catch most people unprepared.

2. What are you doing to prepare for the Lord's return to this earth (v. 11)?

   Discuss actions such as praying, reading the Bible, believing, and repenting.

We should get ready for the Lord's return when he will burn up this world with fire and make a new heaven and earth.

Pray that God would prepare us for his second and final coming, when he will judge this world and bring his people into a new and perfect world.

FRIDAY

1 John 1:1–7 The Cleansing of Sin

1. How does John describe God (v. 5)?

   God is light.

2. How do we know if we walk in the light (v. 7)?

   We have fellowship with other Christians and we are cleansed by Christ's blood.

We enter the light of God and fellowship with other believers through being cleansed by the blood of Christ.

Ask God to shine his light into our lives and through our lives into the lives of others.

SATURDAY

1 John 1:8–2:2 The Confessing of Sin

1. What will happen if we confess our sins (1:9)?

   God will forgive us and cleanse us.

2. What does it mean to confess our sins?

   It means to say the same thing as God says about our sins, to agree with his view of them, and to admit this to him with sorrow.

Confessing our sins to God leads to life and forgiveness not death and judgment.

Confess all our sins to God and find his full forgiveness and cleansing.

SUNDAY

Read the most important verses that your pastor preached on today.

What did you learn about God?

What did you learn about sin?

What did you learn about Jesus?

What did you learn about living?

What is the biggest lesson from the sermon?

What does the sermon lead us to pray for?

EXPEDITION 51
A REVELATION OF JESUS

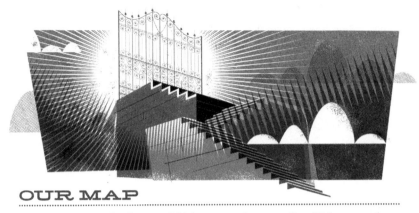

OUR MAP

What a journey we've been on! We've covered many miles. We've seen many countries. We've met many people. We've read many words. But from beginning to end, all these miles, countries, people, and words have pointed to the Savior, Jesus Christ. Yes, we've been exploring the Bible. But we've also been exploring Jesus. We've discovered so much about him from our first expedition in Genesis until now. So you won't be surprised that the last book of the Bible is also full of Jesus. It reveals Jesus to us, especially his love for his church in a hostile world.

 PRAYER POINTS

 SNAPSHOT VERSE
Revelation 1:7

MONDAY

Revelation 1:1–6 Jesus the Faithful Witness

1. How is Jesus described (v. 5)?

   <u>The faithful witness, the firstborn from the dead, and the ruler of earthly kings.</u>

2. What can Jesus do for us (v. 5)?

   <u>Love us and wash us from our sins with his own blood.</u>

Jesus is due honor and glory for who he is and what he has done (v. 6).

Praise Jesus for who he is and what he has done and ask him to be and do this for us.

TUESDAY

Revelation 1:7–11 **Jesus the Beginning and the End**

1. What will happen when Jesus appears again at the end of the world (v. 7)?

   People everywhere will mourn.

2. Why is Jesus called the beginning and the end—the Alpha and the Omega (v. 8)?

   Because he began everything and will end everything.

We must begin and end with Jesus because he is the beginning and end of everything.

Pray that Jesus would be first and last and everything in between in our lives, so that we will rejoice rather than mourn when he returns.

WEDNESDAY

Revelation 1:12–16 **Jesus in the Middle of the Church**

1. What are the seven lampstands that Jesus walks among (v. 20)?

   The seven churches. This is a symbol for the entire church of Christ.

2. What strikes you most about Christ's appearance in heavenly glory (vv. 13–16)?

   Talk through the phrases that describe Christ in glory.

Christ is stunningly awesome and glorious in his heavenly state compared to his earthly state, but still walks among his churches.

Worship the glorious and exalted Christ in all his heavenly glory.

THURSDAY

Revelation 1:17–20 Jesus in His Glory

1. What did John do when he saw Jesus (v. 17)?

   <u>He fell at his feet as though dead.</u>

2. What do Jesus's words to John tell us (v. 17)?

   <u>Jesus told John not to be afraid. This teaches us that Jesus wants his people to enjoy him rather than be afraid of him.</u>

Jesus gives many reasons not to be afraid of him, including that he has the keys to death and life after death (vv. 17–18). This means that he is in charge of both.

Thank Christ that he has the keys to death and life after death rather than some cruel tyrant.

FRIDAY

Revelation 2:1–7 Jesus Speaks to the Loveless Church

1. What had gone wrong in the church of Ephesus (v. 4)?

   <u>They had left their first love.</u>

2. What are the signs of having left Christ as our first love?

   <u>Some examples might be that we have stopped reading the Bible for ourselves, stopped praying, or we are falling into sin a lot.</u>

Jesus wants to be loved first and always.

Pray for unchanging love for Jesus and that we will never fall away from that love.

SATURDAY

Revelation 2:8–11 Jesus Speaks to the Persecuted Church

1. What will Jesus give to his faithful people (v. 10)?

   A crown of life.

2. What does it mean to be faithful to Jesus (v. 10)?

   It means to obey him, follow him, and serve him throughout our lives and even in death.

Jesus notices his people's faithfulness, appreciates it, and will reward it.

Pray for faithfulness to Christ throughout life and for hope of his rewarding crown.

SUNDAY

Read the most important verses that your pastor preached on today.

What did you learn about God?

What did you learn about sin?

What did you learn about Jesus?

What did you learn about living?

What is the biggest lesson from the sermon?

What does the sermon lead us to pray for?

EXPEDITION 52
THE NEW WORLD

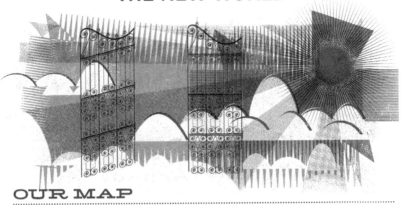

OUR MAP

We started with an expedition to a beautiful garden (Genesis 1). We end with an expedition to a beautiful garden (Revelation 21–22). Although sin entered and damaged the first garden, God has prepared a new garden in the new heaven and the new earth for his people to enter and enjoy forever. In this last expedition through the last two chapters of the Bible, we see a glimpse of the beautiful new world that God has prepared for those who put their faith in Jesus Christ for everything.

 PRAYER POINTS

 SNAPSHOT VERSE
Revelation 22:20

MONDAY

Revelation 21:1–5 The Comfort of Heaven

1. What will Jesus wipe away (v. 4)?

   <u>He will wipe away all tears from our eyes.</u>

2. What are you most looking forward to about heaven?

   <u>Ask all the members of your family what they will enjoy in heaven.</u>

Heaven will have nothing to make us sad and everything to make us happy.

Pray for God to give and maintain our heavenly hope, especially when we are suffering on earth.

TUESDAY

Revelation 21:22–27 The Light of Heaven

1. What will be the light of heaven (v. 23)?

   <u>There will be no sun or moon needed because God's glory and the Lamb's light will make it bright all the time.</u>

2. Who will enter heaven (v. 27)?

   <u>Only those in the Lamb's book of life.</u>

As not everyone gets into heaven, let's make sure we have looked to the Lamb of God who takes away the sin of the world.

Confess our sins and ask the Lamb of God to take them away so that we are written in the Lamb's Book of Life and therefore sure of going to heaven.

WEDNESDAY

Revelation 22:1–5 The Center of Heaven

1. What will we do in heaven (v. 3)?

   <u>We will serve and worship Christ, the Lamb.</u>

2. What will we see in heaven (v. 4)?

   <u>We will see the face of Christ.</u>

Heaven will be a place where we see and serve Christ.

Pray for faith to see and grace to serve Christ here on earth, so that we will see and serve Christ in heaven.

THURSDAY

Revelation 22:6–11 The Nearness of Heaven

1. Who is blessed (v. 7)?

   Those who keep the words of God.

2. What will happen at the end of the world (v. 11)?

   The spiritual state and condition of all people will be fixed forever.

Whether we keep God's word is the test of whether we will go to heaven or hell.

Ask God to help us keep his word so that we will be in heaven forever rather than hell forever.

FRIDAY

Revelation 22:12–17 The Holiness of Heaven

1. What is one of Christ's last words in the Bible (hint: it occurs three times in verse seventeen)?

   Come.

2. How do we respond to Christ's invitation and come to him?

   By putting our faith in him alone for our salvation.

Jesus invites us to come to him for salvation, and reissues that invitation in the last words of the Bible.

Thank Christ for his invitation and come to him for salvation from sin.

SATURDAY

Revelation 22:18–21 The Guide to Heaven

1. What book is Jesus describing (vv. 18–19)?

   The Bible.

2. What does John want his readers to have (v. 21)?

   The grace of our Lord Jesus Christ.

We all need the grace of Christ, the undeserved love and favor of Jesus.

Pray for the grace of Christ to be on us and on all.

SUNDAY

Read the most important verses that your pastor preached on today.

What did you learn about God?

What did you learn about sin?

What did you learn about Jesus?

What did you learn about living?

What is the biggest lesson from the sermon?

What does the sermon lead us to pray for?

THE END OR THE BEGINNING?

Congratulations, you've just traveled the full length of the Bible together with your family and completed a year of daily family worship! Now, of course, we didn't visit every chapter, but we explored the most important peaks in the Bible's story. I hope you and your family agree that the view of God and of his salvation have been worth all the effort.

But what now? Just because you've reached the end of this plan does not mean you end family worship. My hope and prayer is that this is only the beginning, that you've now established such a blessed habit of daily family worship that you will keep it going.

Why not pick one of the Gospels and read it through in the same way as we did in this book? Pray for God's help, read a few verses a day, and ask your family questions about what you've read. Choose a verse to memorize every week. You might want to write these out on small cards so that you can keep them together in a box and review them from time to time.

When you've finished a Gospel, perhaps go to the Old Testament and work through Genesis or the Psalms, then go to the New Testament again, and so on. It's amazing how much Bible you will eventually explore with your family if you read just a few verses a day.

May God guide you and your loved ones deeper into his truth and ultimately deeper into his love.